P9-EEL-220

E. L. Hare

Frontispiece : The
Fokker triplane, the
Dr I, which was
brought into service in
the middle of 1917.

The War in the Air over the Western Front 1914-18

Aces High

Alan Clark

G. P. Putnam's Sons New York

© **Alan Clark** 1973

All rights reserved. No part of this publication may be reproduced,
stored in a retrieval system or transmitted in any form,
or by any means, electronic, mechanical, recording or otherwise
without the prior permission of the copyright owner.

Library of Congress Catalogue Card Number: 72-93663

SBN 399-11103-4

Designed by David Eldred

Filmset and Printed Offset Litho in Great Britain by
Cox and Wyman Ltd, London, Fakenham and Reading

Contents

Appendices

Acknowledgments

Photographs were supplied by and are reproduced by kind permission of the following:

Bettmann Archives: 123; Bibliothek fur Zeitgesch: 59; Chaz Bowyer: 124 (*above*), 127; Culver Pictures Inc: 142, 146; Imperial War Museum: 10, 31 (*below*), 51 (*below*), 52, 54, 55, 58, 77, 79 (*below*), 109, 120, 121, 124 (*below*), 129, 132 (*below*), 135, 139, 151 (*above*), 178, 180, 182; Imperial War Museum (photos by Camera Press): 8, 18-19, 28, 30-31 (*above*), 48, 49, 50, 53, 60, 62-3, 64, 65, 66-7, 68-9, 70, 72, 73, 74, 79 (*above*), 80, 98, 100, 101, 102, 106, 112, 116, 122, 136, 138, 170, 172, 173, 174; Jarrett Collection: 31 (*below*), 105, 119, 124 (*below*), 154; K. M. Molson Collection: 132-3 (*above*); Musée de l'Air: 11, 12, 103, 104, 148, 151 (*below*), 155, 156-7; Science Museum: 13; Smithsonian Institute: 154; Staatsbibliothek, Berlin: 76; Sudd Verlag: 2, 130, 175; Ullstein: 32, 33 (*below*), 108, 114, 181; United Service and Royal Aero Club: 15, 33 (*above*); U.S. Signal Corps: 111, 140, 144, 145; Roger Viollet: 17, 30 (*below*), 34, 46, 51 (*above*).

The diagrams on pages 38, 42, 43, 84, 86, 88, 89, 92, 93, 95, 160, 163 and 168 are by P. Endsleigh Castle and those on pages 41, 44 and 90 are by James Goulding. They are reproduced by courtesy of Profile Publications.

Picture research by Bruce Bernard.

Prologue

Picture if you can what it meant for the first time when all the world of aviation was young and fresh and untried, when to rise at all was a glorious adventure, and to find oneself flying swiftly in the air, the realization of a life-long dream.

Comtesse de Landlot

Everybody who was anybody, the young, the dashing, the adventurous, wanted to learn to fly. But who would teach them? Each individual (and they were not many) who knew something about flying, had his own theories about tuition. Some were sound, others criminally dangerous.

The most popular technique – the 'French School' – was like learning to swim, starting at the shallow end. First the would-be pilots would sit in their aircraft running up the engine and looking around the cockpit in eager bewilderment at the controls while the instructor or some expert well-wisher leaned over their shoulder, blown by the wind, shouting out facts and 'hints' above the roar of the engine. Then the instructor would step down and the pupil would be on his own. He would open the throttle and make the aircraft 'taxi' about on the grass trying (but with little effect for there was no proper airflow over their surfaces) to get some reaction from the controls. At a nod from his instructor, he would increase the throttle opening and the tail would lift, the aeroplane would travel at a considerable speed and perhaps for brief seconds with the more adventurous the wheels would leave the turf, although in theory it was intended that this should be saved for the following day.

An American pupil at the French school gives a vivid account of his experience:

When a student was first learning to crow-hop up and down a field, he'd take off, rise about ten or twenty feet and then bring the ship down almost flat, hardly peaking at all, by blipping the motor on and off. About four or five feet off the ground, the amateur eagle just let her drop ker-wham.

The sound was the general effect of an earthquake in a hardware store, but the miracle was that the ship seemed to suffer no particular ill effects. A tire here or a couple of wires there would go,

Opposite Major F. L. Gerrard flying a Farman biplane past General Sir H. L. Smith-Dorner at the Perham Down Review, May 1913.

RNAS cadet climbing into the observer's seat of a training aircraft for his first flight.

or perhaps a shock-absorber cord, but nothing happened to render the ship unfit for further use.

Gradually the pupil would progress. The aeroplane would be in the air for longer and longer periods at a time and slowly, by trial and error, the pilot would discover how the controls responded. Mechanical waywardness and the frailty of the airframe itself compounded his problems and gradually as he gained altitude, moving into and above the clouds, strange, hidden mysteries emerged.

The importance of wind and air current revealed themselves. Air pockets, caused by sudden fluctuations in atmospheric temperatures, seized the aeroplane and carried it without warning and despite anything that the pilot could do through the engine or ailerons. In the depths of the Salisbury Plain training area a narrow, wooded cleft, some nine miles from Upavon aerodrome, came to be known as the valley of death. Between 1909 and 1913 seven aircraft crashed there, seized on fine summer evenings by its peculiar spiralling air currents and dashed to pieces in the trees. You can visit the place today, unaltered since that time and curiously redolent of its victims' aura.

And then in still air there was another phenomenon. The most frightening of all, and one which for the first two years of the war only a few brave men had mastered, was to exercise a permanent constraint on the airman's inclination to 'stunt' his plane. When a pilot went to make a turn and banked the aircraft over, it would lose speed very rapidly. As the airflow over the wing surfaces diminished – or indeed vanished altogether –

The wreckage of a
Blériot monoplane at
Rheims in 1909.

the controls became lighter and the aircraft's response diminished, speed fell off very rapidly and a stall followed. Then the whole feeling of flight changed. The noise died away, the sound of wind in struts and rigging remained, but took on a new and sinister quality. Over the side of his cockpit the pilot could see the fields, lanes, copses and streams, all the happy panorama of the earth going round, and round, and round. Opening the throttle, making the engine scream, pushing the stick this way or that, was to no avail. Some pilots, very few, discovered in their panic and quite accidentally the correct technique, and lived. But even they found it hard to remember exactly what they had done. The 'spin', when the aeroplane was no longer technically aerodynamic but was simply a large girating kite of metal, wood and canvas, doomed to hit the earth with the force of gravity because it was heavier than air, the element in which it had so insolently tried to move, was the most dreaded plight that could befall an airman.

As there was no cure it was necessary simply to eschew the thought. For three thousand years the only manner in which humans had been able to move independently and at a greater speed than their own legs would carry them, was on horseback. The railway engine ('the iron horse') had given them a kind of confined mobility, and then had come the motor-car, giving them independence also. But to the motor-car at every stage of its development analogies and comparisons with chivalry and the horse had been applied. If anything, the aeroplane with its strange and variable personality, its response to the 'rider's' hands, its temperament, seemed more analogous to the horse than its earthbound predecessor, although both

Air displays and races became popular social occasions in the pre-war years. *Opposite* Poster for a flying exhibition at Rheims in 1909. *Above* Henri Farman, one of the greatest of the French aviation designers, piloting one of his planes at the Rheims exhibition. *Right* Fashionable spectators at the Rheims exhibition.

depended upon the internal combustion engine. No cavalry-man would allow his horse to lie down and roll while he was in the saddle; a touch of the whip (pushing the nose down) would cure an incipient stall. Equally it was a sign of the grossest incompetence – which might have fatal results – if the 'horse' should take the bit between its teeth and gallop, heedless of its rider, in a long and steepening dive. Steady *disciplined* flight was the ideal. 'Stunting' was regarded as dangerous and unnecessary.

Nobody was quite clear about the real purpose of flight – certainly it was not speedy travel, for an express railway train, or even a good Rolls-Royce tourer, was considerably faster. When the military men devoted their minds to it (which was seldom) they thought only in terms of 'observation' – for which requirement, of course, any deviation from straight and level flight was to be deplored.

Yet it is in the nature of man to press into the unknown. The very fact that certain manœuvres were forbidden or fatal lured pilots into attempting them. The first man to fly inverted and survive was a (possibly intoxicated) Russian nobleman, Count Chalakoff. Word spread of his feat among the aero clubs that had mushroomed throughout Europe, and keen and

extravagant competition followed among those who wished to claim the same achievement.

Flying exhibitions became the smartest thing. Many of the wealthy sportsmen who had spent the previous three or four years avidly following the great inter-city automobile races and trying their thunderous Benz and Napier cars down the dusty and deserted Routes Nationales of France, now turned avidly to this new medium. Weekly, it seemed, new feats and experiments were reported. Every step forward was a 'record', a target for those who followed to aim at.

In Britain the link with automobile racing was emphasized by the proximity of the Royal Aero Club (who granted would-be aviators their certificates of proficiency) to the great banked track at Brooklands. The young bloods who fought their 11 litre Benz and Peugeot motors down the railway straight and across the Byfleet Banking, would gather at the Blue Anchor pub and exchange stories with this strange, new, yet enviable breed – the aviators.

Somewhat reluctantly the army establishment began to lay plans for a flying component, which came into existence as the Royal Flying Corps on 13 April 1912, absorbing the previous Air Battalion. Significantly it was accorded only the status of a corps (comprising a Military Wing, a Naval Wing and a Central Flying School), thus ensuring that those charged both with its administration and tactical deployment would be kept in a properly subordinate position and rank. Indeed, it is likely that the army was prompted by its natural rivalry with the Admiralty, who at the instigation of Winston Churchill and others had been quick off the mark in establishing the Naval Air Service, which had been placed under the autonomy of the Admiralty on 23 June 1914 and competed for funds from the Treasury. Until the outbreak of war candidates for the Royal Flying Corps had first to qualify for the Royal Aero Club pilot certificate by taking a civilian course at their own expense (no easy task on a subaltern's pay and leave schedule). Senior regimental officers discouraged their favourites from applying for a transfer and there was an unspoken implication that those who tried for the RFC were unconventional – a serious offence in the military code – or, still worse, 'unsatisfactory'.

After the battles of the Marne and the Aisne, where the airmen had proved their worth but their 'wastage' rate had increased alarmingly, the army undertook to train volunteers to fly *ab initio*. But still the second question in the interview could fail the candidate. The first (to which there could only be one answer) was: 'Why do you want a transfer?' The

second was: 'Can you ride?'

Military instruction was if anything less comprehensible than in the old civilian schools. The chosen mount was the Maurice Farman biplane with a Renault engine known as a 'Shorthorn'. The Shorthorn had certain basic design defects. But knowledge of aerodynamics was still in its infancy and the instructors were too busy or too ignorant to analyse or report on those defects. By trial and error it had been found that some manœuvres induced disaster but it was assumed that the fault lay in the manœuvre rather than in the aeroplane – which had the unfortunate result that a large number of pilots were 'passed out' with an inbred resistance to attempting certain kinds of aerobatics regardless of what their subsequent aircraft might be. The Shorthorn at least had the advantage of dual-controls, but verbal instruction in the air was impossible. The pupil allowed his hands and feet to rest gently on joystick and rudder bars and 'feel' the impulses of his instructor's movement. Some of the latter were intelligent and sympathetic; but as more and more instructors crashed to their death following a pupil's blunder, others of their number

Cavalry and planes before the war. Although most naval and military departments were slow to realize the possibilities of flying, the majority set up experimental departments of military aviation by 1914.

Opposite Above
Maurice Farman
biplane before the
war.
Below Recon-
naissance aircraft
about to depart
in 1914.

came quickly to resent over-confidence or 'ham-handedness'
and would nurture their pupils to the solo stage by the simple
expedient of seldom relaxing their own grip upon the controls.

One recruit gave a vivid description of his first flight:

The nacelle was half-way up the interplane struts. A shallow side
panel hinged down to simplify the gymnastic feat of entering it.
When seated I lifted the panel and secured it with ordinary door
bolts. I was in the nose, well ahead of the wings. The instructor sat
behind, perched between the upper and lower wings' front edges.

Wooden bearers, running aft from the nacelle's structure,
supported part of the engine between the wings and part behind
them where the pusher propeller could revolve. A mechanic
stood within the booms and wires behind the propeller. It was his
unenviable task to help to start the engine from his encaged position.

Before doing anything he first assured himself by question and
answer that the pilot's ignition was switched off and the gasoline
turned on. Then he primed the engine from the carburetter. He did
this by manually rotating the two-blade wood propeller as if he
were himself a starter motor. It was hard work. When he thought
he had done enough he paused and called to the pilot: 'Contact,
sir.'

After the pilot had responded by switching on his ignition and
then announcing 'Contact', the mechanic hopefully and lustily
heaved the propeller a quarter-turn round, while the pilot twirled
a hand starter magneto to boost the spark at the plugs. Usually the
Renault rattled into life after one or two heaves and the
mechanic could emerge from his cage.

This air-cooled V8's pistons had ample clearances. One could
always hear them slapping against the cylinder walls, loudest when
the engine was cold. With no device to compensate for cylinder
expansion and contraction, its valves and tappets chattered
incessantly. Its propeller revolved on an extension of the camshaft
at half engine-speed and the reduction gear was noisy.

The fuel tank, between the rear seat and the engine, was in a
nasty place should a crash occur. The hot engine could break away
from its mounting, rupture the gasoline tank, ignite its contents,
and the burning mass might fall on the aircrew. Fortunately for
their peace of mind, few, if any, pilots or pupils thought about the
several features of the Shorthorn that lowered its safety level
below par. Enough that they were flying! For what more should
they ask?

As for the distinction between military and civilian flying,
this – if its existence was admitted at all – was ignored. Even
the great German General Staff, a body less hostile to new
ideas than its English and French counterparts, had reported
in September of 1914 that: 'Experience has shown that a real
combat in the air such as journalists and romancers have
described, should be considered a myth. The duty of the
aviator is to see, not to fight.'

The 'Roland' Taube, a two-seater mono-plane used by the Germans mainly for reconnaissance. Although superseded by faster and more manœuvrable biplane types, the Taube continued in service up to 1916. The Taube (dove) was so called because of the shape of its wings.

Of the total of thirty-seven aeroplanes that went to France as the advance guard of the Royal Flying Corps nine days after the declaration of the war, none carried armament as part of its specification. The pilot's first task was to keep the aeroplane in the air at all; second, to observe and report back what he had seen. The aeroplane was a 'flying horse' and treated by most of the officers on the Staff with some contempt for the very reason that it was unarmed and also because it could not be properly drilled or 'dressed'. There was also a certain resent-ment among the more orthodox and conservative (always the majority) to this noisy, dirty machine which frightened the *real* horses when it came too close and which was already showing the power of attracting a somewhat 'undesirable' type of officer as pilot. Certainly the new breed, the 'aviators', had much in their make-up to irritate the conventional military mind. Young, full of zest, questioning, with a less than reverent attitude to pomp and discipline, they shared one common characteristic (which is often regarded with suspicion by the military hierarchy, who prefer discipline) – an un-questioned physical courage.

For the first few months of the war the rival aviators would greet each other, on the rare occasions when they met, with a wave of the hand or perhaps some little piece of display to illustrate their prowess, a flick of the wings or a difficult half-roll. The bond which they shared – of being heavier than air and yet moving freely in it by virtue of their own skills – was stronger than the hostility which they were expected to display as soldiers of nations at war. But then, even if the hostility was to remain dormant for a few more weeks or months, a kind of

sporting rivalry began to gather momentum. And as is the case where sport and national prestige run in harness, it became increasingly embittered. On 25 August, three aeroplanes of No. 2 Squadron of the Royal Flying Corps sighted a single German in a Taube observing the French lines of battle. Lieutenant H.D.Harvey-Kelly, the flight leader, dived on the enemy and closed right up on his tail. The German pilot, alarmed by the sudden proximity of this English madman with his threshing propeller four feet from the Taube, dived to get away from him. Harvey-Kelly remained glued to the adversary's rudder. The other two pilots of the flight caught on and joined in the game, one flying on either side of the hapless German. Unable to comprehend what was going on, the unfortunate German pilot put his Taube down in the nearest field. Harvey-Kelly and his brother officers immediately landed themselves, to see the German running headlong to the shelter of a near-by wood. The unarmed Englishmen followed him in and prowled about in the undergrowth for a few minutes without success, then returned to the field where they put a match to the Taube and took off, having recorded the first aerial victory of the war.

How innocent and playful this episode seems when one looks back on it across the headstones of all those graves that were to follow! A rising crescendo for the next four years of all those pilots who were to die with blasphemy on their lips; that were burned, smashed, mutilated, or driven to insanity in a combat that was to become increasingly ruthless and degraded with every month that passed.

Part One

The Opening Shots

Background 1914–15

When the First World War started in August 1914, each of the major powers involved possessed an air force of sorts. Without exception, each was to be shown that the precepts on which she had built up a force of aeroplanes had been not so much wrong as misguided. The most powerful air force was that of Germany, followed by France, with Great Britain's meagre force a considerable way down the list. Each of these three powers, who were to contest the mastery of the air over the Western Front for the rest of the war, considered that the role of the aeroplane was that of reconnaissance, and in a way this was true. Although the world's first heavier-than-air, powered and controlled aeroplane had flown more than ten years previously, and the science of flight had advanced rapidly, the aeroplane was still very much in its infancy. The loads that aeroplanes could carry were still very small, and the carriage of anything more than the crew was a severe impediment to the performance of the machine. To this extent, then, senior army officers, who in all cases controlled the air forces, were correct in stating reconnaissance as the aeroplane's role. But in the long term they were incorrect – they had failed to take into account the rapid rate of growth in the science of flying. Soon aircraft would be capable of longer and faster flight with increased loads, and weapons, offensive or defensive, could be installed. Certainly the most valuable purpose fulfilled by aircraft in the First World War was tactical and strategic reconnaissance; but each side should have realized that the other side would start arming its machines as soon as it could for the very purpose of denying its opponents the chance to spy out troop dispositions, defences and the like, from the air. From this, it should have been deduced that each machine would require some form of defensive armament, and that an arms race in the air would begin. And from spying out an enemy's dispositions it is only a small step to the first attempts to do something about them from the same machine as that from which they were spied; the air would witness the arrival of bombers.

What makes it all the more remarkable that commanders had not foreseen these developments is the fact that the pioneers of aviation had done so. And this they had not done in the seclusion of crackpot attempts at flight, but in the full glare of publicity attendant on the enormously popular pre-war air shows at Hendon, Brooklands, Rheims and the like. Here were prophetic competitions in air attack, as bags of flour, simulating bombs, were dropped on the outline of a dreadnought battleship laid out on the airfield. In addition to this, machine-guns were taken into the air in attempts to arrest the attention of the military – in Britain Major H.R.M.Brooke-Popham was censured by his commanding officer for endangering his Blériot by attempting to get a machine-gun on it; in the United States, Colonel Isaac Newton had experimented with his famous air-cooled machine-gun in a Wright biplane, but had been so discouraged by the authorities' lukewarm reception of the idea that he had left his native land and started up his own manufacturing concern for the gun in Belgium in 1913. In France, the more far-sighted army had let the aircraft manufacturer Raymond Saulnier borrow a machine-gun to experiment with an interrupter gear to allow a stream of bullets to pass through the disc swept by the propeller without hitting the blades; and in Germany Franz Scheider of the LVG concern was conducting experiments along the same lines. In both of the last two cases, the authorities lost interest after a few early reverses.

No matter what more imagination might have revealed, the air forces of 1914 were geared almost exclusively to reconnaissance. The largest air force was that of Germany, which had 246 aircraft and seven Zeppelin airships, with a total air crew of 525. This comprised the Imperial German Military Aviation Section. (It is worth noting at this point that the Imperial German Navy Air Service had thirty-six aircraft and two Zeppelins.) With considerable forethought, the German High Command had instituted a sizeable expansion programme, but this was geared to too great an extent to lighter-than-air craft. These appealed to the military partly for patriotic reasons, as Germany led the world in the development of this kind of machine; partly as a sop to the enormous enthusiasm engendered in the German people for the type as a result of Graf von Zeppelin's early tribulations and later success with lighter-than-air craft; but mostly to the Zeppelin-type's enormous potential as a strategic reconnaissance craft, with very large range and considerable ceiling. This ignored the basic failing of the airship, however: extreme vulnerability because of its very nature – an elongated balloon filled with highly inflammable hydrogen gas.

The most common heavier-than-air type in service with the German Air Force was the Taube (dove), a shoulder-winged monoplane of Austrian invention made in large numbers by several German manufacturers. These comprised about half the 246 aircraft owned by the German Air Force, the rest being made up mostly of biplanes of the LVG, Aviatik and Albatros types. These aircraft were formed into forty-one Fliegerabteilungen or flight sections, the basic German unit for aircraft. Each Abteilung *had a nominal strength of six machines, and of the forty-one sections, thirty-four were* Feldfliegerabteilungen (Flabt) *or field flight sections, assigned to the operational control of army and corps commanders, while seven were* Festungs-fliegerabteilungen *or fortress flight sections, assigned to the protection of the seven major German fortress towns along her borders. These last had a strength of four aircraft. Control of equipment and personnel was exercised by the* Inspektion der Fliegertruppen (Idflieg) *or Inspectorate of Flying Troops under Major Wilhelm Siegert. The growth of the importance of the air force was reflected by the establishment, on 11 March 1915, of the office of the* Chef des Feldflieg, *whose first occupier was Major Hermann Thomsen.*

The French Air Force, *or* Aviation Militaire, *had a strength of 160 aircraft and fifteen airships at the beginning of the war. The airships were mostly of the Lebaudy type and the aeroplanes of Blériot, Voisin, Morane-Saulnier, Farman and Deperdussin types. The basic organization was into* escadrilles *or squadrons of six aircraft each in two-seater units and four aircraft in single-seater units. Command was exercised by the Directorate of Aeronautics at GQG, the French Army High Command. Head of the Inspectorate was Commandant Barès, later succeeded by Commandant du Peuty. One of the handicaps suffered by the French Air Force derived, perversely, from France's pre-eminent position as producer of most of Europe's aircraft. There were thus so many types in service that maintenance was a very severe problem. Luckily for Britain, this strength in manufacturing capability enabled France to sell many machines to her ally at a time when Britain's own aircraft industry was still trying to gear itself to the production needs of a long war.*

It is worth noting two major differences in design theory between the French and the Germans, derived from the basic power units available in each country. The French had been the inventors of the best pre-war type of engine, the rotary, and in the two forms of the Gnome and the Le Rhône it powered the majority of France's best early machines. Its advantage lay in an excellent power-to-weight ratio, and its light weight was combined with compactness. However, its development potential was not as good as that of the type favoured by the Germans, the water-cooled inline. This type was at a disadvantage vis-à-vis the rotary in the first two years of the war, but with a few exceptions proved to be the better power plant in the long run as it was capable of greater development. Derived from this, German aircraft design, for the most part, concentrated on well-streamlined, strong, heavy and fast machines, whereas the French favoured light, agile machines with a good rate of climb. It must be pointed out, however, that the best French fighter of the war was an inline-engined type, the Spad XIII, and that some of Germany's most important fighters, notably the Fokker E I, Fokker Dr I and Fokker D VIII, were rotary-engined, often with Gnomes or Le Rhônes salvaged from crashed French machines.

Military flying in Great Britain was in the hands of two bodies at the beginning of the war. The force that travelled to France with the British Expeditionary Force was part of the Royal Flying Corps, an army formation. Left behind to guard Britain's shores was the Royal Navy's air force, the Royal Naval Air Service.

The basic RFC unit was the squadron of three flights of four aeroplanes each, higher units being the wing and the brigade. RNAS basic units were flights, squadrons and wings. At the beginning of the war Britain could call on 113 aeroplanes and six airships; of these, sixty-three flew to France with the BEF in August 1914. The main types were the BE 2 series, Avro 504s, Farmans of various marks and several Blériot XIs. The whole force was under the command of Major-General Sir David Henderson who was succeeded on 19 August 1915 by Hugh Trenchard, then a Lieutenant-Colonel.

These then were the air forces available to the fighting powers in the western theatre in 1914. The Germans had a numerically strong air force, with an enormous potential. The French were numerically weaker, but had a better long-term manufacturing capability. The British were in the worst position. Their manufacturing capabilities were in the short term poor, and many machines had to be imported from France. Apart from that, machines were in short supply and to a great extent outdated (as were many German types) and the force was starved of funds. In operational doctrines, France led the field, recognizing the three distinct needs of reconnaissance, artillery co-operation and bombing long before the British and Germans.

French superiority was made abundantly clear when aircraft moved into action in 1914, for it was French machines that scored all the 'firsts' in strategic reconnaissance, properly organized bombing and air fighting. The first occurred on 3 September, when French airmen spotted the increasing gap between the German First and Second Armies approaching the Marne, which led to the Allied victory that halted the German advance. (British airmen had achieved a notable coup, however, in the field of tactical reconnaissance, spotting the German outflanking movement during the Battle of Mons on 22 August, and also the French withdrawal.) The second occurred on 14 August when French Voisins attacked the Zeppelin sheds at Metz; and the third occurred on 5 October, when a mechanic named Louis Quénault, in a Voisin piloted by Joseph Frantz, shot down a German Aviatik two-seater with the Hotchkiss machine-gun mounted in the nose of his pusher type. The first example of bombs being dropped was by a German Taube over Paris on 13 August, but the missiles in this instance were only for propaganda. The first successful instance of artillery co-operation, however, was by the British, during the Battle of the Aisne in mid-September.

As can be seen from the above, the aeroplane had quickly proved its worth in war. The French immediately set about organizing a strategic bomber force equipped with Voisins, and all three nations realized fully the need for a fighting aircraft which could prevent enemy machines coming across to observe behind one's own lines, and also protect one's own machines when on reconnaissance flights. The first attempts to produce such a machine had been made as 'private enterprise' inventions within the ranks of the squadrons' more enterprising pilots, but later these gave way to properly designed fighters, though initially the absence of adequate interrupter or synchronizer gears was an almost insuperable handicap. The early efforts utilized whatever any particular pilot or observer could lay his hands on – pistols, rifles, shotguns, grenades (suspended below the aircraft and intended to detonate on contact with one's opponent's machine) and even machine-guns – if they could be obtained – on home-made mountings. The trouble with the first four, even had they been practical, was that there was no adequate way of aiming; and with the last that there was no way of firing directly ahead of the aircraft. Moreover, the weight of the gun made it probable that the enemy machine would escape before the pursuer got into range, if it ever did so. Another problem was that posed by the design of the aircraft. Most two-seaters were tractor biplanes, with the observer's cockpit forward of the pilot's, compassed about by the wings, wires, propeller and other impediments to both the handling and the firing of the gun. The only other sort of two-seater, the pusher, gave the observer a much better view from the front of the nacelle, and also gave him an unimpaired forward field of fire, but performance was so hampered by the design, however, that the enemy had an excellent chance of escaping before his pursuer came in range.

It has been claimed, with some justification, that the world's first fighter was a British machine answering to the above description, the Vickers FB 5 'Gunbus', the first of which arrived in France on 5 February 1915. It was also this type that formed the equipment of the first fighter squadron to be supplied uniformly with the same type, No. 11, which arrived for service in France on 25 July 1915. Previously, as the squadrons had all been intended as reconnaissance units, they had been equipped with a miscellany of general purpose types, squadrons receiving twelve examples of a single type wherever supplies permitted. But with the advent of fighting machines, it was deemed advisable to attach to each squadron one or two 'Scouts', single-seaters whose function it was to protect as best they could their more cumbersome two-seater brethren. The day of air forces made up of entirely homogeneous squadrons, though, was still a long time off. For the time being, the British and French had to make do with the protection afforded by their Morane-Saulnier Ns, Nieuport 10s, Bristol Scouts and Sopwith Tabloids. At about the same time, Spring 1915, the Germans were introducing a new class of aeroplane, the 'C' class, which was to remain in service for the rest of the war. The requirement for this class was for an armed two-seater biplane of more than 150 h.p., to fulfil the general purpose role. This class eventually included good machines such as the Albatros C I, DFW C V, Rumpler C IV and Halberstadt C V. Moreover, the Germans displayed considerable forethought and decided to build four classes of fighting machine. These classes were to fulfil the tasks of bombing, aerial fighting, ground support, and reconnaissance and artillery spotting. In this they were far in advance of any Allied planning.

However, more momentous changes were in the offing. The first true single-seat fighter, the Fokker E I, was about to emerge, and with it the 'Fokker Scourge'.

CHAPTER ONE

Airmen

Flying alone! Nothing gives such a sense of mastery over mechanism, mastery indeed over space, time, and life itself, as this.

A hundred miles, north, south, east, west. Thirty thousand square miles of unbroken cloud-plains! No traveller in the desert, no pioneer to the Poles had ever seen such an expanse of sand or snow. Only the lonely threshers of the sky, hidden from the earth, had gazed on it. Only we who went up into the high places under the shadow of wings!

Cecil Lewis

The romantic isolation of the airmen was something real and exalting. They were separate and above the verminous squalor of the trenches, the prolonged ordeal which they touched occasionally when flying low over the lines, or when being brought back from a forced landing at the front. Hearsay and rumour magnified the horrors of perpetual siege warfare, living underground, the butchery of the 'Pushes', the reek of ether and gangrene in the hospitals. There were very few cases of officers opting for a transfer back to their regiments once they had served in the RFC.

But for this very reason the Flying Corps was totally neglected by the High Command in terms of amenity and recreation. The 'indiscipline' of the flyers was a source of continual irritation to the Staff – the more so since squadron commanders tended (it seemed) to connive at it. In tacit recognition of the freemasonry that grows between aviators, it was thought preferable that the senior officer responsible should be someone who did not fly and as a result many interesting technical innovations, particularly in the field of gunnery, which the pilots attempted to introduce from their own experience, were forbidden as being against regulations.

Those forward airfields were bleak, lonely places – cinder runways cut through acres of beet and kale. Fire-fighting and medical services were minimal and the returning injured or those who suffered from accidents at landing or take-off would have to endure a ride in a Crossley tender to the nearest field hospital, often as much as thirty minutes distant. At night the ground shuddered from gun-fire and the eastern sky flickered

Manfred von Richthofen preparing for a flight. He is wearing the sheepskin boots which pilots found so necessary, fighting at altitudes where the temperatures could be many degrees below zero, even in June.

Opposite A new recruit arriving for training with the RFC.

white and violet. Leave schedules were arbitrary and those lucky enough to survive in combat could be kept in station for months at a time. Of recreation there was little variety – only the forced jollity and maudlin aftermath of the 'binge' which would begin at dusk and continue often until those taking part were insensible.

A DH 2 'pusher' biplane taking off from the forward airfield at Beauval in Northern France.

Uniformity of clothing deteriorated. Regimental tunics, RFC 'maternity jackets', sweaters, silk scarves, woolly scarves, leather flying coats buttoned up or falling loose, sheepskin boots, knee-length flying boots of fleece-lined leather with suede tops, slacks and shoes, or breeches and puttees – all these were worn on operations or about the mess to the fury of inspecting 'brass'.

There was very little entertainment in the evenings. No radio or 'shows'; only what music the squadron itself could make or extract from clockwork gramophones that had to be cranked by hand between each 78 r.p.m. disc. Musical taste varied from one unit to another, setting its own conditions. Some preferred hits from the London shows whose tunes evoked glimpses of home and leave; others sang the bawdy or tragic ballads of the RFC's own songs; whilst a few established a tradition of 'classical only'. It was expected of every squadron member who went on leave that he should return with at least one gramophone record for the mess.

Squadrons had no padre, no church parades. They flew every single day that weather permitted, and lost count of weeks and weekends. Drunkenness varied from one unit to another, and with the fortunes of battle. During a bad run aircrew on dawn patrol would sometimes not go to bed at all

Opposite A French aviation section billeted in the hills outside Rheims, 1915.

German propaganda postcard commemorating Max Immelmann, one of the first generation of aces who emerged in 1915. He joined an air unit in November 1914 and in March 1915 was passed as a pilot. After his second encounter with an enemy aircraft on 3 June he received the Iron Cross. He went on to score fifteen victories, earning the title of 'Eagle of Lille' before his death in June 1916.

or only for a short period of stupor, with ill effect on their flying ability (although pilots soon discovered that a hangover could be temporarily cured by ascending over 8,000 feet).

It was in these early months of 1915 that the first generation of aces emerged. The term and title really belongs to 1917, the year of the circuses and the great mass dog fights that would break down into individual contests of skill, judgment and bravery. But in 1915, when men like Major Lanoe G. Hawker, Lieutenant Max Immelmann and Oswald Boelcke made their mark, the machine itself was still suspect; its fickleness was still the first enemy.

Gunnery – whether from the ground or from hostile aircraft – was occasional and erratic. Combat tactics were nebulous and experimental. It was the frailty of the airframe and the unreliability of the engine that were the prime restraints on a pilot's enterprise. Manœuvres which, in theory, the pilots could work out for themselves as being ideal for evasion, were nevertheless avoided for fear of stripping the fabric, or tearing out the stay wires at their roots. Few men who sheared their wing struts or lost a rudder lived to tell the tale; practical experience in the true sense of the term was unobtainable, and rumour of a particular aeroplane's strange failings and weaknesses would spread quickly through the squadrons and deter all but the most intrepid from putting it to the test. It could happen that an aeroplane which was seen to break up in the sky had already been weakened by enemy bullets. No one could know for certain. It was only in the heat of combat when a few brave men discarded prudence that these things could be put to the test.

Often it was the case that pilots who were the least skilful or intrepid were hardest on their engines. Long pursuit dives after an escaping foe would allow engine revolutions to build up over the safety limit, ultimately with critical results – overheating, damage to valves and pistons and sometimes total failure. Few early aircraft were fitted with more than a fuel supply gauge and an oil pressure indicator. Pilots had to rely on their own sensibilities, ears, nostrils and 'feel' to tell them of the engine's health. Some of them, of course, were grounded in mechanics. They were fascinated by the internal combustion engine and responded naturally to its vagaries. But for all those young cavalry officers who joined the Flying Corps in preference to a dismounted posting to the trenches, oil temperature, compression ratios, valve overlap and such terms were pure double-dutch and best left to the 'troops' (as the mechanics were called).

During this period squadron equipment was not uniform,

Left An attempt to mount a gun on an English plane in 1912.

Below Oswald Boelcke, one of the first and greatest of the German aces. He had already scored forty victories by October 1916. His early successes were partly due to being chosen to fly one of the first of the Fokker 'E' series monoplanes.

but each unit was a hotchpotch of different types of aircraft suited (if the word is not too ironic) to different tasks. In the squadron the most glamorous and desirable were the single-seater Scouts, now beginning to make their appearance. In due course No. 6 Squadron, where in 1914 one of the earliest experiments in mounting a machine-gun on an aeroplane (a Farman) had been tried by Lieutenant Louis Strange, received its first single-seater, a Martinsyde Scout. Major Gordon Shepherd, the Commanding Officer, acceded to Strange's fervent plea that he should be allowed to fly the plane.

Strange was an experienced pilot (and, as will be seen, a very brave man also) and he soon found that the Martinsyde had a combination of several vices which, although individually often found in aircraft of this period, were usually accompanied by some compensating virtues. It was slow, unstable and yet lethargic in its response to the controls – in other words the very opposite of what was required in combat against other aircraft. Its only virtue was that it mounted a forward-firing Lewis gun on a fixed mounting above the upper wing.

Mechanics in an aircraft repairing shed in France.

Undeterred by the Martinsyde's tricky handling, Strange headed due east and was soon well inside enemy territory. After some time he spotted his prey, an Aviatik flying above and to the north of him. But to close with his enemy took an age. The weight and drag of the Lewis gun cut the Martinsyde's speed to less than 6o m.p.h. in its shallow climb. When the observer of the Aviatik alerted his pilot it too struggled to gain altitude. Soon Strange found that his adversary was drawing away from him. The Martinsyde had reached its ceiling and could climb no more. Drawing the joystick back, Strange lifted the machine's nose and fired a long deflecting burst at the enemy, emptying the Lewis gun. Serenely the Aviatik flew on.

Strange was angry, and disappointed; now he began to feel afraid also. The chase had led him far behind the enemy lines; it had brought home to him how useless was the Martinsyde in combat; the magazine of the Lewis gun was empty and he was effectively defenceless. Strange put up one hand to unclip the magazine so that he could reload. He was now in a gentle dive back towards the front line twenty miles to the west, with an air speed of some 75 m.p.h., and could expect to be over friendly territory in a quarter of an hour. But the drum was stuck and the pressure of the wind made it very difficult for Strange to grip it firmly with his gloved hand. He throttled right back and lifted the nose to reduce air speed. Still the empty drum remained obstinately stuck to the breech. Strange removed his gloves, then stood up in the cockpit cursing with all his might and straining with both hands to twist the magazine against its spring-load.

But now the Martinsyde, which had slowed almost to stalling speed, performed one of its most objectionable antics. The port wing dropped sharply. Strange lost his balance and fell against the joystick, giving instant full left flap, which exaggerated the aeroplane's spontaneous manœuvre and turned the machine upside down. In the space of two seconds Strange found that he was hanging like a trapeze artiste with both hands still on the magazine of the Lewis gun while the Martinsyde flew hesitantly above him in an inverted position. Now his curses that the drum should free itself changed to prayers that it should hold. The thread (only one and a half circuits of 360 degrees) had crossed. All that was holding Strange's weight of 150 lbs was a $\frac{1}{4}$ mm. width of low tensile steel that surrounded the magazine attachment. If this broke or if the drum freed itself, as he had been trying so hard to make it do for the last ten minutes, Strange would have fallen, still clutching the empty magazine, some 9,000 feet to his death. By an incredible feat of physical prowess – which involved putting even greater strain on the jammed magazine – Strange hauled himself up the distance of his elbows and started a series of desperate swings, any one of which might have dislodged the drum, to try and hook his legs inside the upper (now the lower) wing of the Martinsyde. At the third attempt he succeeded in doing this, but his violent shifting of weight and the slowly declining air-speed had caused the Martinsyde to go into a spin.

At this early stage in the techniques of aerobatics the spin was regarded as virtually incurable – as a long but inevitable prelude to certain death. For Strange it was particularly and immediately objectionable in that while he was trying to haul himself back into the cockpit against the force of gravity, he had also to fight against the horrible giddiness which builds up in the spin and which was, of course, aggravated by the fact that he was upside down.

By now the Martinsyde had lost some 7,000 feet of its original altitude of 9,000 feet. How Strange managed to hook his feet back into the rudder controls remains incredible – still more how in the remaining 1,500 feet or so he managed to correct the spin and right the aircraft, a feat little short of miraculous. In a very shaken condition he flew the Martinsyde back to the aerodrome at tree-top level, and on landing was charged by the Commanding Officer with causing 'unnecessary damage' to the instruments and seat (by kicking them with his feet while trying to climb back into the cockpit).

Part Two

The Weapons are Forged

P ENDSLEIGH CASTLE ARAeS ©

Fokker E III

Background 1915–16

The winter of 1915–16 was the 'Fokker Scourge'. It began when Fokker, in the summer of 1915, delivered his Eindekker with its single Parabellum machine-gun mounted on the cowling. No Allied aircraft could stand up to the Eindekker because of its fire-power. The aeroplane itself was structurally weak and possessed of an indifferent performance as it was, even in the E III mark, underpowered. But, luckily for the Allies, the Germans issued it in ones and twos to reconnaissance and other squadrons much as the British issued Scouts. Had the Germans formed homogeneous units of the E types in 1915–16, they must surely have driven the air forces of the Allies from the skies.

This is not to say, though, that some enterprising individuals had not made the attempt to gather together enough to make a particularly devastating weapon. In the late summer of 1915, an officer in the Bavarian Air Force, which was partially independent of the rest of the German Air Force, made such an attempt and formed three Kampfeinsitzerkommando, *or single-seat fighter units. Two of the pilots in the second of these were Oswald Boelcke and Max Immelmann. These two were portrayed as rivals in the German press, and though they may have been so, Boelcke's importance was far greater than Immelmann's. For while Immelmann's greatness lay in being one of the first fighter aces, that was his only achievement, as he was killed after scoring fifteen victories. Boelcke, however, achieved forty victories, but much more than that, he was the father of aerial warfare. He taught, developed tactics and in every way laid the foundation of the science of aerial fighting.*

The place where Boelcke and Immelmann rose to fame was Verdun, where the Germans were trying 'to bleed the French army to death'. Inadvertently, they produced the world's first large scale fighter unit – on the French side. This was the Cigognes, *the élite French fighter force of the First World War. In the early summer of 1916 they were equipped with the little Nieuport II Bébé fighter, whose Lewis gun, firing over the top wing, went part of the way to wresting control of the air from the Fokkers. It was soon joined by the Spad VII, which had a synchronized Vickers gun, and the combination soon wrested superiority from the Germans over the southern part of the Western Front.*

To the north, the British were also making headway against

German air power. Even at the height of the Fokker Scourge, Trenchard had insisted on sending out as many aircraft as possible on offensive patrols, and this proved enormously expensive in lives and machines. The tactics have been severally criticized, as the machines were decidedly inferior to their German counterparts, and the pilots, a large percentage of them straight from flying school with no combat experience, were unable to cope with the radical change of tactics needed to cope with the E series. Those who did not come back had become 'Fokker Fodder'. On 27 February 1916, however, No. 24 Squadron arrived in France. It was equipped with the first British single-seat fighter, the De Havilland 2, and was under the command of the third airman to win a Victoria Cross, Major Lanoe G. Hawker. The DH 2 was a pusher, as Britain still had no synchronizing gear, but it was agile, and so more than a match for the Fokker. The tide was beginning to turn. Fighting alongside the DH 2 was the cumbersome but immensely strong FE 2, which also proved itself capable of dealing with the Fokker. And from May the French started supplying Britain with the Nieuport II, when they could afford to let their Allies have them.

With the arrival of these new fighters, the RFC started to develop offensive tactics as a means of defending two-seat reconnaissance machines, which were still a very ineffectual breed on the Allied side. For example, early in February before No. 24 Squadron had become operational, a BE 2C on a reconnaissance sortie had had to receive an escort of no less than twelve other machines. RFC doctrine still stated that fighters should defend general purpose machines from a position of close escort, but enterprising pilots realized that it was more efficient to go and 'look for the enemy than wait for him to find you'. Thus were born the offensive fighter tactics that took the Allies over the German lines during the rest of the war. Even when the tide was running against it, the RFC was to be found on the east of the lines.

As the year progressed, moreover, the superiority which the Allies now enjoyed was further enhanced by even better machines. On the British side, the excellent Sopwith $1\frac{1}{2}$ 'Strutter' two-seat fighter/reconnaissance machine, equipped with a synchronized Vickers for the pilot and a Lewis for the observer appeared early in the year, easily the best two-seater on either side so far. It was joined in September by the delightful Sopwith Pup, a scaled-down single 'pup' of the $1\frac{1}{2}$ Strutter. And the French supplemented the Bébés of their Escadrilles de Chasse with an updated version, the Nieuport 17, from March onwards.

The Germans were also developing new types, notably the Halberstadt D series in autumn 1915 and spring 1916, the Fokker D I in the summer and the Albatros D I and II with its new twin gun armament, in the autumn. With the last, Germany

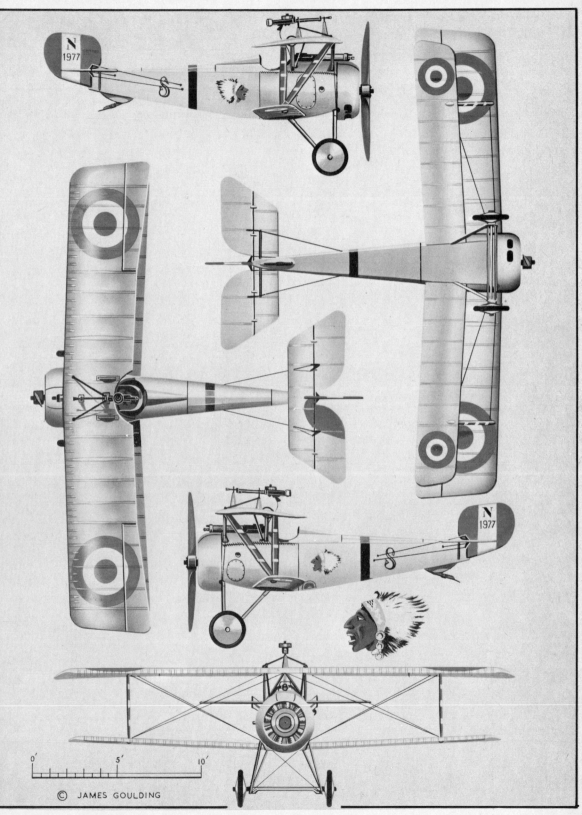

Nieuport 17

0'   5'   10'

© JAMES GOULDING

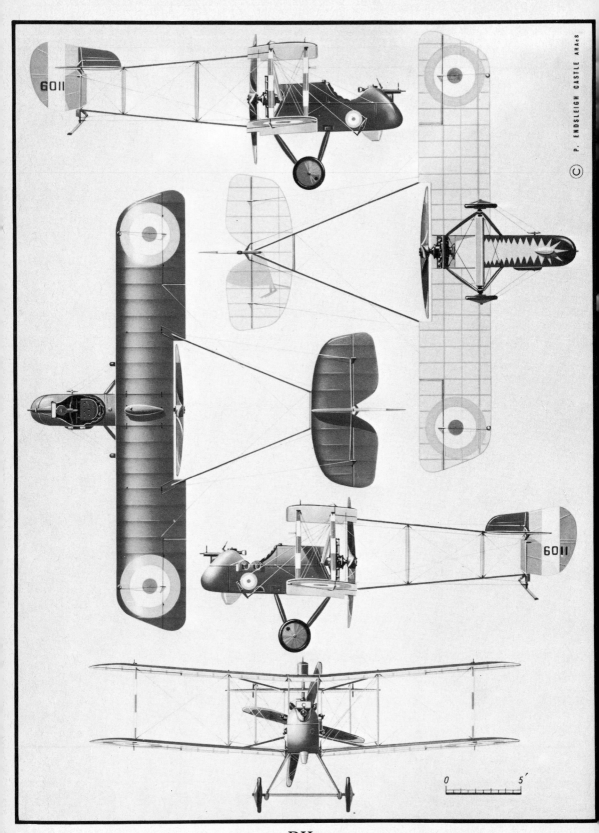

© P. ENDSLEIGH CASTLE ARAeS

DH 2

FE 2B

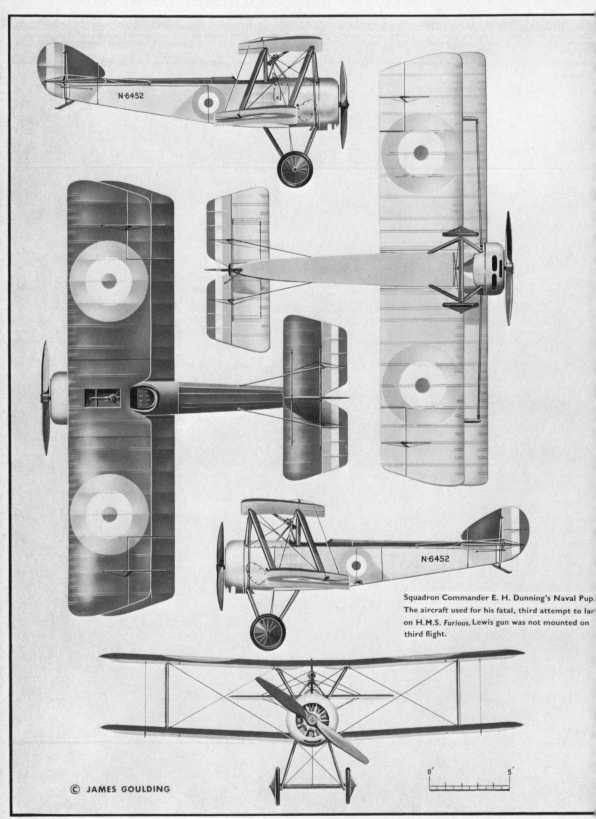

N·6452

N·6452

Squadron Commander E. H. Dunning's Naval Pup. The aircraft used for his fatal, third attempt to land on H.M.S. *Furious*. Lewis gun was not mounted on third flight.

© JAMES GOULDING

0'   5'

Sopwith Pup

again began to gain the ascendancy over the Western Front.

Not only German machines, but also German organization and tactics had undergone changes in the summer and autumn of 1916. First of all, the lessons of the Kampfeinsitzerkommando *had been digested. Then, in August, a new tactical fighter unit of fourteen aircraft, the* Jagdstaffel (Jasta) *or fighter squadron, was introduced. Boelcke had long been in favour of this, and he was given command of the first one to be formed,* Jasta 2. *This became operational in September 1916 and, by April 1917, thirty-seven had been formed. But on 28 October 1916, Boelcke himself, the father and mentor of the idea was killed in an air accident, when he collided with another member of his* Jasta, *which was later renamed* Jasta Boelcke *in his honour. Boelcke's lessons had been well learnt, however, as the original members of his* Jasta 2 *were soon commanding successful* Jastas *of their own. One of these was the youthful Manfred von Richthofen, who commanded* Jasta 11.

Another event of importance for the German effort in the air was the establishment of the Deutschen Luftstreitkrafte *or German Air Force. This was set up on 8 October 1916, and its first commander or* Kogenluft *was General Ernst von Hoeppner, with Hermann Thomsen, now a colonel, as chief-of-staff and Wilhelm Siegert as* Idflieg. *Returning to the tactical aspect of the German reorganization, it is worth noting that an event overshadowed by the arrival of the Fokker, but hardly less important, was the development of German infantry support tactics, or contact patrols. In the absence of any type of 'walkie talkie' radio in the First World War, divisional corps and army commanders found it very difficult to keep track of the position of their forward troops during an attack, and consequently also in gunlaying or any form of support by other ground troops or artillery. Thus aircraft came to be used for the task of establishing contact with forward units, as in the Battle of Verdun. An elaborate system of visual codes was arranged, and each division had its* Fliegerabteilung Infanterie (Fl. Abt. - Inf.). *At first, ordinary C class machines such as the* DFW C V *and* LVG C II *were used, but their extreme vulnerability to ground fire soon led to armour plate being fitted around the engine, fuel tanks and crew compartment, while proper armoured contact patrol aircraft (the J class) were designed. The idea was soon copied by the Allies.*

The scene was now set for the next major development in aerial fighting. The Fokker Scourge had risen and eventually been beaten, and while the new generation of Allied fighters, the SE 5, Sopwith Camel and Spad XIII, was being developed, the Germans put the sleek, shark-like Albatros D I and II into service, and were about to introduce the even better D III 'Vee-Strutter', which was to bring about the decimation of the RFC during 'Bloody April'.

An early attempt at
mounting a gun on a
French aeroplane in
February 1914.

Machines

Take the cylinder out of my kidneys,
  The connecting rod out of my brain, my brain,
From the small of my back take the camshaft
  And assemble the engine again.

RFC Mess Song

In those days designers were still inhibited by the development of the engines that drove their craft. The majority looked upon their product as a sailplane with its own motive power, rather than as a projectile containing a man and a gun. An aeroplane is by definition something heavier than air. The designers were at pains to keep this disparity as low as possible, and the results were two-fold: while the human body is so constructed that it cannot sustain fatal injury in a collision at any speed up to the maximum of which it is capable under its own motive power, this was very far from the case with the early aircraft. Of course they could never be expected to resist collision with other objects, but they did not even have the strength to hold together under the maximum stresses which a skilled pilot could impose upon them in the air. Long dives would strip the fabric from the wing surfaces; tail planes would shear in a zoom or too tight a turn. Undercarriage gear would snap on contact with the ground if the angle of approach were misjudged.

But as compensation for these failings, the aeroplanes did possess a delightful buoyancy. Their take-off and landing from rough and sloping grass fields were, by today's standards, quite incredible. They could glide a considerable distance if starting from some altitude and this saved many lives; for although the engines were unreliable the majority of pilots became proficient at handling their aeroplane down to the nearest grass patch in a 'dead-stick' condition. Often at the end of a day's mission, pilots would turn off the engine at a great height after crossing their lines and guide the aeroplane down, gently losing height through the evening sunlight with only the sound of wind in spars and rigging.

In terms of military technology, the evolution of the machines passed through four distinct stages, and with each

Morane monoplane fitted with a deflector airscrew. The major problem of fitting a machine-gun on the fuselage in a position where it could easily be aimed by the pilot was that at the same time it was in a position to strike the propeller blades. One solution was to fit metal plates to the blades which, hopefully, would deflect the bullets.

development complete ascendancy passed to whichever side had anticipated it.

At first the aeroplane was used solely for intelligence 'Scouts' – a description which later indicated what were, strictly speaking, single-seat fighters. The aeroplanes were in most cases unarmed and if by chance they should meet in the sky they would ignore each other. Their enemies were the weather, the imperfect skill of the pilots, and their own structural weaknesses, and, a long way behind these three, occasional bursts of inaccurate groundfire from hostile (or friendly) soldiers.

But very quickly the ingenuity and enthusiasm of the pilots began to extend the role of the aeroplane into the second stage of its evolution. The crews would take up revolvers or stalking rifles and take pot-shots either at hostile aircraft or at enemy soldiers on the ground. Some of them would take up hand grenades or eighteen-pounder shells fitted with makeshift fins and when they had crossed the enemy lines they would lean over the side of the aeroplane and drop the missiles by hand. It was only a matter of time before machine-guns began to find their way into aeroplanes, though initially only as the observer's weapon on two-seaters.

But the machine-gun was a heavy weapon and it consumed a lot of ammunition. Moreover, its field of fire was severely restricted by the structural outline of the aeroplane itself, particularly by the airscrew which, in front-engined aeroplanes, made it impossible to use a machine-gun except in the three-quarter rear field. Plainly the first designer who could combine a forward-firing machine-gun and a high speed single-seater aircraft, would enable the squadrons thus equipped to establish an immediate superiority over the more unwieldy two-seaters with their restricted fire.

One of the chief difficulties in designing an interrupter gear was that ordinary machine-gun ammunition did not have a precisely uniform period of ignition; hand-fire rounds would occur unpredictably, and if the pilot was out of luck these would strike his airscrew. As early as 1913, a German, Franz Schneider of the LVG, had designed an interrupter mechanism and taken out a patent. However, for some reason the German military authorities refused to supply him with a machine-gun on which to run field tests. In the meantime Raymond Saulnier had been conducting parallel experiments in France. Saulnier had become impatient with hang-fire failures and had circumvented this by fitting steel deflection plates on the propeller blade where its arc crossed the line of the gun; and this device, though clumsy, was none the less a great advance. But, as in Germany, the military authorities lost

German two-seater
observation plane
showing a Parabellum
machine-gun and
mounting.

interest at the outbreak of war and made Saulnier return his gun.

Gears to allow a machine-gun to fire through the disc swept by the propeller fall into two categories – the interrupter and the synchronizer. The former works on the following principle: when the trigger is pressed, the machine-gun fires, and when the propeller moves into its line of fire, a series of mechanical linkages operated from the propeller interrupts the action of the gun until the propeller blade is out of the line of fire. In the latter, when the trigger is pressed, nothing occurs until the propeller is safe, and then the engine-driven gear, either mechanically or hydraulically, completes the circuit necessary to make the gun fire.

After three months of war, the pilots were unanimous in their desire for freedom to fire fixed machine-guns in the direction of flight. For they had soon realized that it was difficult enough to fly the aeroplane at all, and keep out of trouble in combat, without having repeatedly to alter course and execute manœuvres at the bidding of the 'gunner' who was trying to get the enemy aeroplanes in his sights. If the pilot by aiming the aircraft could also be aiming the gun, his task would be greatly simplified and his speed of reaction doubled.

Lieutenant Roland Garros, who had been a famous stunt pilot before the war in Morane-Saulnier monoplanes, visited Raymond Saulnier in December of 1914 and arranged to have his own aeroplane fitted out with the new device for a forward-firing machine-gun. The interrupter gear was not fitted, Garros relying on the deflection plates only to ward off the bullets that would otherwise have struck his airscrew. The

Lewis gun mounted in the nacelle of an FE biplane. The Lewis gun was invented by an American, Isaac Newton Lewis, and was mounted on the early fighter planes. It had serious drawbacks on single-seater planes: the gun was not within easy reach of the pilot if it developed a blockage during flight; and to replace an empty drum the pilot had to stand up in the cockpit.

work proceeded at a leisurely pace and it was not until the end of March that Garros took to the air. But his success was immediate and electrifying. In just over a fortnight he had shot down five German aeroplanes – an unprecedented score for that period. But on 19 April he was brought down by ground fire while strafing a column of enemy infantry on a road near Courtrai. Garros' attempts to set fire to his aeroplane were unsuccessful and the Germans immediately set about copying and modifying it.

On the evening of the day following Garros' downfall his armoured airscrew was already in Anthony Fokker's workshop being mated to a brand new Parabellum machine-gun. By 20 May the Fokker team's adaption of the device into a true interrupter gear had been fitted to two of his new single-seater monoplanes (Fokker M 5K) and these were sent on a demonstration tour of operational units.

Max Immelmann, at that time an unknown squadron pilot at Douai, wrote:

We have just got two small one-seater fighters from the Fokker factory. The Crown Prince of Bavaria visited our aerodrome to see these new fighting machines and inspected us and Section 20. Direktor Fokker, the constructor of this fighter, was presented to him. Fokker and a Leutnant Parschau gave demonstration flights for him and fired at ground targets from the air. Fokker amazed us with his ability.

And by the first week of July eleven of the leading German pilots were flying Fokker E 1 single-seaters, derived from the M 5K, equipped with the forward-firing Parabellum. Their effect was as dramatic as that of Garros' – only multiplied tenfold.

In these early days of aerial combat, pilots had been conditioned to believe that they were immune from enemy bullets when their adversary was bearing directly down on them. For too many their last visual memory on earth was of the little orange flickering that appeared above and very slightly to the right of the Fokker's propeller boss as it opened fire.

The appearance of the Fokker transformed the balance of power in the air. For some months there was literally no answer save that of swamping the enemy by sheer numbers – the counterpart of 'stopping bullets with bodies' on the ground – or, in rare cases, where the pilot could utilize superior flying skill to evade pursuit.

For example, the log of No. 12 Squadron shows that an escort for one reconnaissance BE 2C was made up of three other BE 2Cs, four FE 2Bs, four RE 8s and one Bristol Scout. This was an extraordinarily cumbersome and wasteful way of

Roland Garros, the French aviator who was the first to fit his plane with Saulnier's new device for a forward-firing machine-gun.

Anthony Fokker, the brilliant young Dutch designer, who invented the synchronized machine-gun (with the help of Saulnier's deflector airscrew which had fallen into German hands).

The famous Fokker EI fighter fitted with a Spandau machine-gun on top of the fuselage and fired with the Fokker interrupter gear. With this plane, the German Air Force obtained superiority over the Allied air forces in the winter of 1915/16.

operating the air arm as all these aircraft except the FE 2B, which had a Lewis gun for the observer in the front of the nacelle, were virtually incapable of engaging in combat with the Fokker, much less of actually overcoming it. (Moreover, the date of this particular escort, 7 February 1916, is not associated with any particular incident or period of activity on the ground and it is unlikely that the reconnaissance was of more than routine importance.)

Had the Fokkers been more numerous and had the Germans deployed them in greater concentration it is probable that the RFC would have been faced with annihilation. Fortunately for the British, however, the bulk of the Fokker strength was drawn south to the battlefields of Verdun and the RFC was allowed a breathing space while it awaited the arrival of a new generation of aircraft.

The Fokker's real strength lay in its unique ability to fire through the propeller; the aeroplane itself was somewhat frail and underpowered. The torsional strength of a single wing was dangerously inferior to that of a trussed biplane, and the wires and the upright upper and lower pylons on the fuselage with which Anthony Fokker had tried to brace the wing surfaces were vulnerable both to hostile fire and to the exceptional buffeting which might follow a violent manœuvre or pulling out of a dive.

These characteristics gave the Fokker an awesome reputation among the German pilots. In July 1915 some of the production aircraft were sent to the flying school at Doberitz for use as training aircraft. On 27 July one crashed fatally, and a second Fokker pilot was killed on 31st. After a third Fokker

Pilot seated in the cockpit of a DH 2 with a Lewis gun mounted in the nose. The DH 2 was not an outstanding fighter plane, being neither particularly fast nor manœuvrable, but it was superior to the Fokker Eindekkers and gained a certain ascendancy in the summer of 1916.

fatality on 29 August the *Idflieg* disbanded the Doberitz Fokker unit, sent the aircraft back to the Fokker works at Schwerin, and grounded the monoplanes as service aircraft. However, the Fokker's success at the front was so marked that the *Idflieg* was compelled to allow the resumption of training, but they stipulated that it was to be done at the Fokker flying school at Schwerin. The first group of trainees were sent there from Doberitz in October 1915.

Furthermore, the 100 h.p. Oberursel engine could only just drive the Fokker at 80 m.p.h. and the production of the 160 h.p. engine which raised its maximum to 100 m.p.h. was extremely slow. Several Fokkers were fitted with captured 92 h.p. Le Rhône engines which greatly improved their performance (and emphasized the somewhat theoretical quality of the Oberursel's claimed 100 h.p.).

In the spring of 1916 the Fokker myth began to disintegrate. The first of the Nieuports (the Nieuport II, or *Bébé*) had made their appearance in the skies over Verdun and as their numbers rose so did the Fokkers become more and more chary of battle. In the north the British had captured one and found that:

. . . it was perfectly orthodox, and there remained only to put it up against a British Scout to judge its performance. The Morane Bullet was chosen, and the two machines were run out on the aerodrome, side by side. All the General Staff assembled to watch the test. Both machines took off together, and it was immediately clear that the Morane was all over the Fokker. It climbed quicker, it was faster on the level, and when the two machines began a mock fight over the aerodrome, the Morane had everything its own way.

The Sopwith 1½
Strutter, the first
British aeroplane to
carry a forward-firing
gun with a
synchronized device.
It was soon outclassed
by the arrival of the
German Albatros D I
fighter.

A cheer went up from the ground. The bogey was laid. A description of the machine, its size, power, capabilities, was circulated at once to everyone in the Corps. It did a great deal to raise the morale and prepare the way for the Allied air supremacy later that year.

The third stage of evolution coincided with the Battle of the Somme, through the long, baking summer of 1916. British output of aircraft had increased in spectacular fashion as also had recruitment into the RFC. Although still hampered by lack of a powerful purpose-built engine, the Royal Aircraft Establishment had managed to purchase a consignment of second-hand French engines which they fitted to their new airframe, the DH 2. The DH 2 was a 'pusher' of the old box-kite configuration that had killed so many trainees in 'Shorthorn' form and was soon to become obsolete, acquiring an evil and somewhat undeserved reputation among the line squadrons as the 'spinning incinerator'. But for a few months the DH 2 did attain a kind of ascendancy. Its rear-mounted engine allowed a clear field of fire for the Lewis gun in the nose and, more important, an unrestricted *rate* of fire. (For all interrupter and synchronizing devices greatly restricted the gun's rate.) The tactics of the RFC during this summer were, in aerial terms, the counterpart of Sir Douglas Haig's repetitive frontal assaults on the ground. But thanks to the diversion of the Fokkers southwards, the symbolic victory of an FE 2B gunner named Corporal J.H. Waller over Immelmann on 18 June 1916, the dash and courage of units such as Lanoe Hawker's No. 24 Squadron, they did succeed in establishing

a transient supremacy – although at a high cost in lives.

Yet the principles of the DH 2 design were obsolete before it was even put into service (and indeed were to remain so until the advent of the jet engine which applies its power in 'thrust' from the rear instead of 'pull' from the front). The French had already seen the importance of a front-mounted engine from the point of view of speed and manœuvrability; once sufficient power could be developed to lift two machine-guns, the 'pusher's' faster rate of fire would be more than discounted.

A few lucky RFC pilots, among them such future aces as Albert Ball and James McCudden, managed to get their hands on the latest French scout built to this principle, the Nieuport 17. Almost as fortunate were the flyers in the RNAS who were being issued with the tiny but phenomenally agile Sopwith Pup fighter.

The first British aeroplane to carry a forward-firing gun with a synchronized device, was another Sopwith, the $1\frac{1}{2}$ Strutter. This also had a rearward-firing gun for the observer, as it was a reconnaissance fighter. The $1\frac{1}{2}$ Strutter had only a short life as a dominant weapon before the arrival of the first true two-gun fighter, the German Albatros D 1, which completely outclassed it. The Strutter was then relegated to bombing and reconnaissance roles, but the pilot loyalty it inspired was intense: 'They were delightful aeroplanes to fly and beautiful to look at. On the ground when taxi-ing to take-off, they looked like brown butterflies; in the air they were alive and full of grace, charming companions of the clouds.'

The $1\frac{1}{2}$ Strutter had a single machine-gun fitted with the Ross interrupter gear that restricted its rate of fire to 300

The Nieuport 17, an updated version of the Nieuport *Bébé*, was brought into the service in the summer of 1916. Its chief distinction over the *Bébé* was that it was armed with a synchronized Vickers gun in addition to the Lewis on the top wing. The British Nieuports, however, retained the Lewis gun as the only standard armament.

rounds per minute (compared with over 1,000 rounds per minute from the Albatros' twin Spandaus). In addition, the Ross gear was very prone to jamming. However, the earlier examples left the normal ground trigger on the Vickers so that in a really tight corner the pilot could squeeze this and double his fire power at the risk of shattering his airscrew.

Perhaps the plane's gliding and handling ability encouraged this drastic expedient. The messes of $1\frac{1}{2}$ Strutter squadrons were plentifully adorned with whole and sheared propeller blades. The beautiful wood, laminated walnut or mahogany, was often carved into ornaments, tobacco jars, mounts for clocks and barometers.

Charm, sweetness, agility, all these qualities were possessed by the Sopwiths and the Nieuports and made them beloved of their pilots. But in a fighting machine these qualities are not entirely pre-eminent. In Germany a perfect fighting machine – the Albatros D – was under development, and from the date of its first appearance it flaunted an absolute superiority, until, nearly a year later, the antidote had been contrived. This Albatros marked the beginning of the fourth stage in the evolution of fighting machines.

The Albatros D series machine was a beautiful and deadly biplane. Developed from the same builders' successful series of reconnaissance machines and some special plywood-covered racing planes of the pre-war era, it was fitted with the 160 h.p. water-cooled Mercedes engine which allowed better streamlining (and thus higher speed in dive and climb) at the expense of some slight reduction in manœuvrability. Its twin Spandau machine-guns gave it the highest rate of fire of any aeroplane in service at that time. Furthermore, the impact of the Albatros was magnified by the way in which the Germans deployed it. Instead of distributing them a few at a time all along the front, they were grouped in *Jagdstaffeln* (abbreviated to *Jastas*) or 'hunting squadrons' whose express purpose was to seek out and destroy enemy aircraft – i.e. without the constraint of escort, reconnaissance, and other missions.

The double impact of this deadly new aeroplane and the manner in which it had been entrusted to picked groups of élite flyers was to cut a wide swathe through the ranks of the Royal Flying Corps in the months that followed. Many of its bravest pilots, the gifted and imaginative pioneers of its early formation, officers who might have played critical parts in its expansion, were to perish under the guns of the Albatros.

If the passing of the Fokker's ascendancy was symbolized by the death of Immelmann, then it is still more true to say that the lethal advent of the Albatros was marked by the long and gruelling final encounter between the man destined to be the ace of aces of the First World War with eighty victories, Manfred von Richthofen, and Lanoe Hawker.

Of all the early fighting pilots, it was Lanoe Hawker who had the supreme mastery of his machine. He was a superlative shot and in the earliest days had mounted a Westley Richards .300 single-shot deer-stalking rifle on a rigid bracket outrigged to clear the airscrew, and with this antiquated weapon had managed to score several confirmed destructions. So perfect was Hawker's aim and so beautifully co-ordinated were his touch and judgment at the controls of the aircraft, that he could fire a single deflection shot with the deer-stalker that would wound a vital part of the enemy engine or penetrate the skull of its pilot. His victories against machine-gun-armed planes had to the enemy a mysterious and terrifying quality for their planes seemed just to fall out of the sky for no reason. Used to the deadly clatter of machine-gun fire, they could not hear that single, fatal crack above the roar of their own engines and the sound of adjoining combat. By the time that the second generation of 'pusher' aeroplanes arrived that were to sweep the Fokker Monoplane from the sky over the Somme, word had spread through the whole German air service of this remarkable Englishman with the moustache who could make his aeroplane perform such prodigies of manœuvre and evasion.

But time passed, development advanced, the sleek and speedy Albatros arrived on the scene in ever increasing numbers. The DH 2s had to fight ever harder and their obsolescence became daily more apparent. Only Hawker's incredible flying skill saved him from death when cornered by groups of German pilots flying new machines. Twice he was shot down and once wounded. With each week that passed the strain increased. The moment from which there could be no escape drew nearer.

How unbelievable it is that this brave and talented man should have been condemned to fly one patrol after another in machinery that had become totally out-classed – the very counterpart in the air of that extravagant and obstinate butchery that was repeatedly being ordered on the ground, where brave men were being sent to certain death in pointless and repetitive attacks on the same strongpoint. The gradual decimation of Hawker's valiant No. 24 Squadron and his own ultimate fate are still less excusable when it is recalled that the instruments which might have allowed them to survive, namely the new Sopwith Triplane (or even the agile little Pup itself) were being flown by the RNAS in the northern sector of the front where the Germans respectfully gave them a wide berth.

Hawker's fame among the enemy was such that all the pilots of the newly forming *Jastas* were eager to pit their skill against him (though whether they would have been so keen had he been known as the pilot of a Triplane is another question). During the winter months of 1916, several had the opportunity and some did not survive the encounter. But then at last on 16 November, Hawker fell in with Richthofen – a man cunning enough to avoid, even for a split second, the kind of error that would give Hawker the opportunity either to exploit his brilliant aim or to himself escape the clutches of the Albatros. Again and again the two aircraft turned in near vertical bank. Each time Hawker's skill and delicacy in throttling back at the apex of the turn and allowing the DH 2 to side-slip for brief seconds, caused him to slide out of the German's sights at the critical moment. Then briefly Hawker could put the nose of the DH 2 down in a dive, and seize a few precious yards of direct flight homeward. But sickeningly soon the superior power of the Albatros allowed it to catch up and the deadly turning process was repeated. For each time that Hawker weaved his way out of Richthofen's sights, he lost precious altitude, and each time that he lost altitude he used up his reserve of speed and distance for the bolt home.

After what seemed an age – fifteen, twenty minutes – the duellists were at ground level, the DH 2 could turn no more. Desperately Hawker weaved and soared round tall trees and over farm buildings. Once an air pocket wafted the DH 2 vertically some precious hundred feet and Hawker could dive again. But the last seconds of his life were ebbing away. The Albatros stood off at a distance of about sixty yards, waiting. This time there would be no escape. As the Albatros closed in for the kill Hawker gave full left rudder in a last despairing effort to bring his nose round and meet his enemy head on. But Richthofen opened his throttle and the enormous margin of power in the Mercedes engine drew the Albatros on top of its target, now at maximum exposure and almost motionless in its steep bank. One long burst raked across the engine and on Hawker's head, shoulder and knees. The DH 2 fell like a stone, bursting into flames as it hit the ground.

Manfred von Richthofen; 'When I have shot down an Englishman my hunting passion is satisfied for a quarter of an hour.'

Opposite Major Lanoe Hawker, the first and one of the greatest of the British aces, who fell to Richthofen's guns on 23 November 1916.

CHAPTER THREE

Tactics

If by some delightful chance,
　　When you're flying out in France,
Some old Boche machine you meet,
　　Very slow and obsolete,
Don't turn round to watch your tail,
　　Tricks like that are getting stale;
Just put down your bally nose,
　　And murmur, 'Chaps, here goes!'

(To the tune of 'Tonight's the Night')

Even the most experienced pilot could be surprised, particularly if his attention had been absorbed by a target on the ground or stalking another enemy at a lower altitude. In that first instant when the hammer blows of a Spandau burst rocked his fuselage, only immediate rudder, joystick and throttle forward in a steep diving turn could save his life. It had to be a reflex action. The inexperienced would 'freeze' in terror or waste precious fifths of a second looking round left and right to see where the enemy was coming from.

The pilots of the single-seaters could thus save themselves even after being surprised and come back to fight again (though with the disadvantage of a lower altitude). But for the two-seater it was different. Heavier, more stable and slower, their response was less agile and usually their pilots were less experienced in combat, being trained for ground observation and navigation. For their protection they depended upon the observer and his ring-mounted machine-gun (Lewis or Parabellum). But the observer, too, had duties to perform – duties which were at their most pressing when the aircraft was over the target area, that is, when the danger of interception was also at its most critical.

For a high altitude interception the most favoured tactic was to approach the two-seaters from below and to the rear where the 'blind-spot', particularly when the plane was in straight and level flight, would effectively mask the assailant. When the scouts attacked in pairs the technique was for one to distract the observer's attention, usually by a broadside attack, opening fire at very long range, while the killer approached from below

Opposite In 1918 the RFC started to put out diagrams to help new pilots to get to know the sort of tactics to expect in combat. Far too often in previous years pilots had gone to the Front not knowing what to expect. This diagram shows three German planes pursuing a British Scout.
Overleaf Diagram showing how to attack an enemy two-seater.

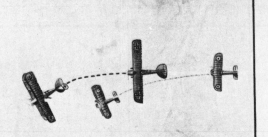

INCORRECT METHOD.
THE NATURAL INCLINATION OF THE ATTACKER,
IF INEXPERIENCED, IS TO TURN IN THE SAME
DIRECTION AND FOLLOW.
    THIS RESULTS IN GIVING THE ENEMY JUST
THE OPPORTUNITY HE DESIRES.

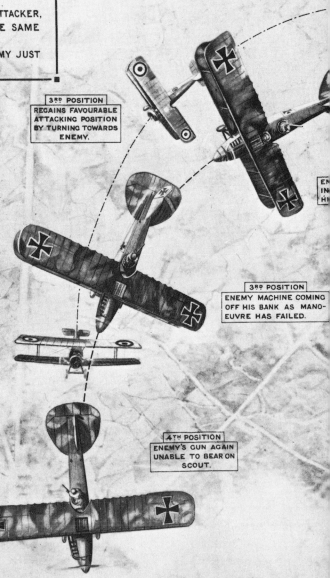

3ᴿᴰ POSITION
REGAINS FAVOURABLE
ATTACKING POSITION
BY TURNING TOWARDS
ENEMY.

EN
IN
H

3ᴿᴰ POSITION
ENEMY MACHINE COMING
OFF HIS BANK AS MANO-
EUVRE HAS FAILED.

4ᵀᴴ POSITION
ATTACKING MACHINE
AGAIN IN POSITION
UNDER ENEMY'S TAIL.

4ᵀᴴ POSITION
ENEMY'S GUN AGAIN
UNABLE TO BEAR ON
SCOUT.

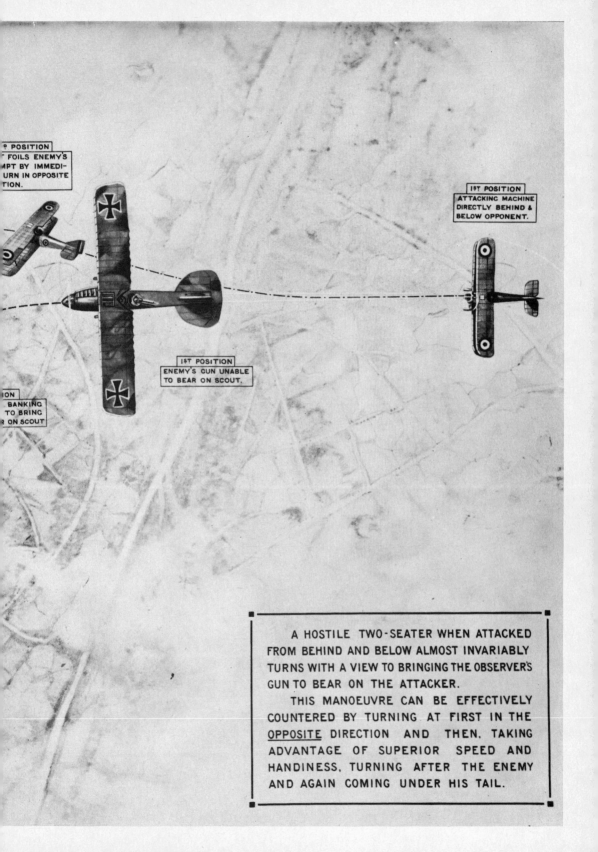

2ⁿ POSITION
FOILS ENEMY'S
[ATTE]MPT BY IMMEDI-
[ATE T]URN IN OPPOSITE
[DIREC]TION.

1ˢᵀ POSITION
ATTACKING MACHINE
DIRECTLY BEHIND &
BELOW OPPONENT.

1ˢᵀ POSITION
ENEMY'S GUN UNABLE
TO BEAR ON SCOUT.

[POSIT]ION
[STEEP] BANKING
[IN ORDER] TO BRING
[GUN TO BEA]R ON SCOUT

A HOSTILE TWO-SEATER WHEN ATTACKED
FROM BEHIND AND BELOW ALMOST INVARIABLY
TURNS WITH A VIEW TO BRINGING THE OBSERVER'S
GUN TO BEAR ON THE ATTACKER.

THIS MANOEUVRE CAN BE EFFECTIVELY
COUNTERED BY TURNING AT FIRST IN THE
OPPOSITE DIRECTION AND THEN, TAKING
ADVANTAGE OF SUPERIOR SPEED AND
HANDINESS, TURNING AFTER THE ENEMY
AND AGAIN COMING UNDER HIS TAIL.

Diagram showing the dangers of an enemy plane attacking 'out of the sun' with the help of a decoy plane.

closing the distance to the optimum figure of thirty metres.

Where a single-seater was attacking by itself, it would normally do so in a dive out of the sun, although accurate positioning of this kind took considerable flying experience and a high degree of concentration. Towards the end of the war the habit spread among rear gunners of mounting a sheet of mirror to swing in parallel with the gun ring and if this could be focused accurately even for a split second, it would completely dazzle the attacking pilot.

The extra speed and agility of the single-seaters should have made it easy for a skilled pilot to pick off his very cumbersome adversary more or less at will. Furthermore, the majority of two-seater crews were relatively inexperienced, and had received only a brief theoretical background to the finer points of air-to-air combat. Yet the fact remains that a team of skilful pilots and gunners with steady nerves could be very formidable. Many of the highest-scoring aces – Guynemer, Richthofen, Lufbery – fell victim to a resolute rear gunner.

Tactical skill was a composite of many things. Awareness of clouds and wind; private deceptions and bluff; cool nerves and speed of reaction; above all, flying skill, sensitivity to the aircraft's response, which involved complete knowledge of acceleration, rate of roll, climb and turn and height-holding ability, and keen vision. This last was as much a matter of experience and intuition as of pure physical efficiency. There was a certain way of looking at the ground or sky, a manner of focusing, which allowed experienced pilots to notice the minute and menacing specks of hostile aircraft; and until this had been mastered, all novices were at risk.

Spring and early summer of 1917 – that period when the RFC suffered most grievously under the flail of the Albatros Circuses – were marked by much cloud.

Diagram of an aerial battle between Fokker Dr Is and DH 9s.

To the early airmen cloudland was a new world. To the imaginative few, it became an enchanted land, the fairyland of childhood dreams come true.

To the fighting airmen clouds were significant above all else. They meant the chance to stalk and trap, but carried also from within their soft and towering cliffs, the threat of being taken by surprise. Skilled pilots learned how to fly just within the cloudfringe. Invisible from below and yet able themselves to scan the sky beneath them. It was important to know in evasion how soon a cloud would give cover for a sudden change of course. Pilots learned to estimate the strength of clouds, their size and direction, whether they were growing or diminishing.

On three days out of five the west wind prevailed, and fights that started at altitude would, as the contestants lost height, gradually work their way over the fighting zone and deep into German-held territory. Speeds even at maximum, were low and the differentials correspondingly small. In level flight, few aircraft had a margin of more than ten or fifteen m.p.h. over their enemy. Anyone who has driven a car fast over an empty, undulating road and tried to catch and overtake another of similar performance some little distance ahead, will have an idea of the closing pace in aerial combat in the First World War. Judgment and experience were vital in determining the angle of dive in a pursuit; if too steep, the attacker might pass below his intended victim and lose precious time in climbing

Overleaf Diagram showing good and bad looping.

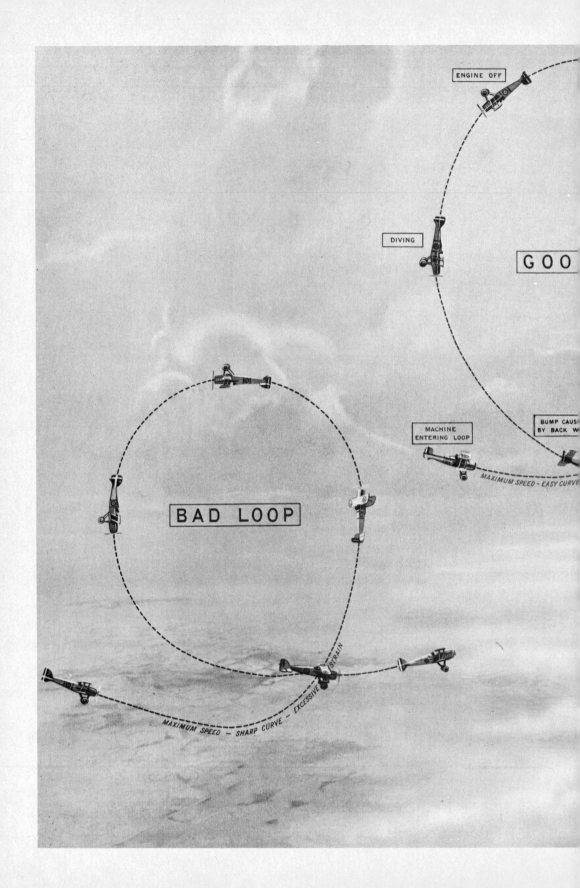

ENGINE OFF

DIVING

G O O

MACHINE
ENTERING LOOP

BUMP CAUS
BY BACK W

MAXIMUM SPEED - EASY CURVE

BAD LOOP

MAXIMUM SPEED - SHARP CURVE - EXCESSIVE STRAIN

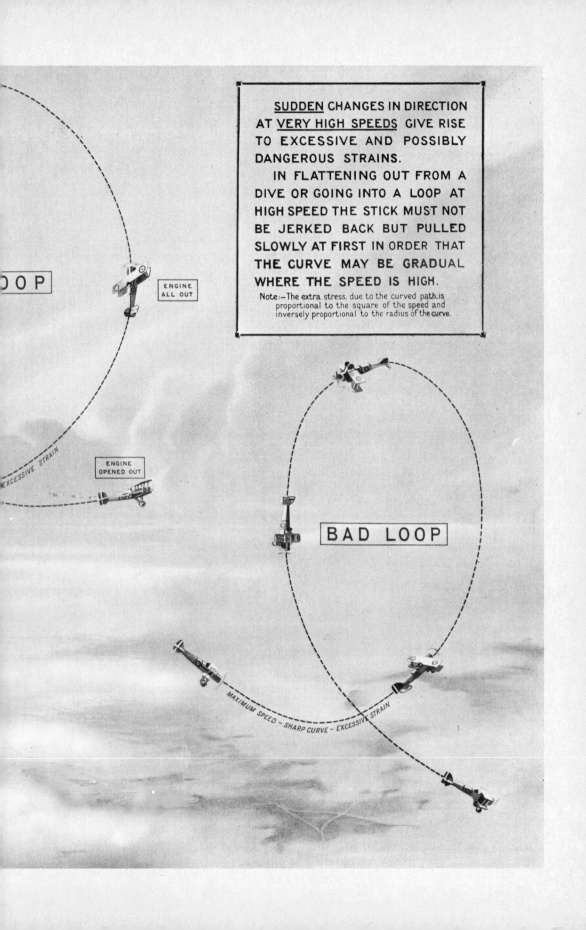

SUDDEN CHANGES IN DIRECTION
AT VERY HIGH SPEEDS GIVE RISE
TO EXCESSIVE AND POSSIBLY
DANGEROUS STRAINS.

IN FLATTENING OUT FROM A
DIVE OR GOING INTO A LOOP AT
HIGH SPEED THE STICK MUST NOT
BE JERKED BACK BUT PULLED
SLOWLY AT FIRST IN ORDER THAT
THE CURVE MAY BE GRADUAL
WHERE THE SPEED IS HIGH.

Note:—The extra stress, due to the curved path, is
proportional to the square of the speed and
inversely proportional to the radius of the curve.

OOP

ENGINE
ALL OUT

EXCESSIVE STRAIN

ENGINE
OPENED OUT

BAD LOOP

MAXIMUM SPEED – SHARP CURVE – EXCESSIVE STRAIN

again; if too shallow, he might alert his prey before closing within range and it too would have time in which to start diving.

A number of the German *Jasta* pilots (Lothar von Richthofen, Werner Voss and many others) had started their careers as observers and knew the kind of tricks that would upset a two-seater crew. If he thought his enemy might escape, Richthofen would open fire early, in short bursts, and the nervous two-seater pilot would start premature avoiding action, thus fatally slowing his own plane and allowing the enemy to close to a proper striking distance.

By the time Bloody April of 1917 came round, the very high

IN CASE OF ENGINE FAILURE
DON'T TURN BACK — PUT HER NOSE
DOWN AT ONCE AND MAKE SOME
SORT OF A LANDING AHEAD.

3RD POSITION.
MACHINE OUT OF CONTROL
SPIN COMMENCING.

4TH POSITION.
SPINNING NOSE DIVE.

5TH POSITION.
CRASH.

Diagram showing
what not to do in case
of engine failure.

casualties which the two-seaters were suffering had left few
crews with proper combat experience. The army's insistence
on continuous 'offensive' patrols and the total obsolescence
of their equipment were causing squadron casualties of
approximately thirty per cent per week. For example, Manfred
von Richthofen's log for 13 April 1917 shows a certified claim
for an FE 2B at 8.58 a.m., 12.45 p.m. and 7.35 p.m. on that
day – i.e. on each of his three patrols. Yet in his total score,
Richthofen only included three SE 5A single-seaters, not
claiming the first one until 30 November 1917, more than six
months after they became operational.

PANCAKING CONSISTS
STALLING THE MACHINE J▨
ABOVE THE SURFACE OF ▨
GROUND AND DROPPING ▨
REMAINING 2 OR 4 FEET W▨
AS LITTLE FORWARD SPEE▨
POSSIBLE.

A PANCAKE LANDING ▨
MADE ON ROUGH GROUND, ST▨
-ING CORN, WATER ETC., WHER▨
ORDINARY LANDING WOULD ▨
ULT IN A SOMERSAULT.

THE ILLUSTRATION IS IN▨
-DED AS A WARNING AGAINST ▨
-CAKING FROM TOO GREAT A HE▨
OR LANDING ABOVE THE GROUND▨
OPPOSITE ERROR OF ATTEMPT▨
TO LAND BELOW THE GROUND▨
OF LESS FREQUENT OCCURRE▨
THOUGH IT MAY BE MORE DIS▨
ROUS IN ITS RESULTS.

1ST POSITION
MACHINE HAS FLATTENED OUT
TOO SOON – PANCAKING FROM
TOO GREAT A HEIGHT.

2ND POSITION
NOSE HAS FALLEN &
MACHINE CRASHED.

IF GROUND LEVEL HAD BEEN HERE MACHINE WOULD HAVE LANDED CORRECTLY.

ACTUAL GROUND LEVEL

Diagram showing the dangers of a 'pancake' landing from too great a height.

The Germans could not understand the way in which the British aeroplanes daily came over the lines to be shot down. 'It is better if the customers come to the shop', was Richthofen's dry comment. 'Certainly they are brave, but it is bravery that has a touch of foolishness about it.' Combat against the French he dismissed lightly: 'In a Frenchman, bravery is quite exceptional and if you do meet it, it is like a glass of lemonade and very soon goes flat.'

With every adversary against whom a pilot actually duelled (as distinct from surprising out of the blue and killing at one stroke) he established a kind of personal relationship – the shape of his head, his grimaces under stress (many of the best pilots would not wear goggles for these restricted at the corners the eye's natural field of vision), how strong was his nerve, how merciful or deserving mercy – and there is little doubt that this contributed to the neuroses of remorse or vindictiveness that gradually unbalanced the aces.

Norman MacMillan has given a vivid account of his first meeting with Werner Voss, just after the latter had been issued with one of the new Fokker triplanes:

I saw the triplane curve in behind his tail [McMaking, another pilot in MacMillan's Sopwith Camel Squadron] and dived instantly at it. Before my sights were centred I fired a brief burst because I knew most Huns reacted to the warning sound of bullets flying near them. This fellow, however, was of a different breed. He looked round at me and I saw his black leather helmeted and begoggled face above his left shoulder as he swerved slightly to one side then looked ahead again and followed the Camel's tail.

I think McMaking must have been wounded by the triplane's first fire, because he did not use his Camel to manœuvre as he might have done. He went down straight in a steepish dive, with no attempt at evasion.

I increased speed and pulled closer to the triplane. I was now below the main Hun formation and I heard the splatter of Hun bullets rattling round my ears. Glancing back and upward I saw two Albatros coming down upon me, but above them, Moody, in another little Camel, was treating them just the same and driving them off.

Now I was almost dead upon the buff-coloured triplane's tail. Its pilot looked round again. Possibly the sound of the bullets his comrades aimed at me had alerted him. I was close enough to see (and almost read the expression in) his keen blue-grey eyes behind his goggle glasses and as much of his face as was left uncovered; nose, mouth, chin and shape of cheek. Had I been able to meet them I could have picked him out from among his fellow pilots.

He saw I was dead on his tail and instantly banked and curved to the right while he looked at me just as my bullets spewed forth. My tracers passed close over his central left wing, just outside his cockpit and in line with his head, missing it by inches because of his outward swerve. When my brief burst ceased he looked ahead again. He was a clever pilot.

I saw McMaking's Camel still below him, falling steeply in a gentle curve. If he were already badly wounded (as I believe) why did his opponent not leave him to his fate and turn to duel with me? We were at an advantageous height for the Fokker Triplane for both climb and manœuvre. Did he think the Camel ahead of him might escape across the lines? Or was it his policy to butcher him right to the ground in order to claim his scalp? I was alone now, our odds were even, and we were on his side of the lines, an advantage to him. Surely he ought to have rounded to engage me? I have never understood his tactics, why he did not take me on . . .

In the last resort flying skill at the limit of feasibility was critical. For it was this above all else on which the pilot's life depended. Tactics worked out in theory, demonstrated on a blackboard, practised in the still and friendly air of Salisbury Plain, broke down in the stress and turmoil of combat. Then the pilot's reflexes, the sixth sense that led him to respond to his aircraft's whims and protests, were everything. When the wing surfaces or the fuselage were damaged or the engine was

Pilot officer firing at a
fixed target from a
'cockpit' moving along
rails at an RAF
gunnery school in
France in July 1918.

misfiring, the joystick sluggish – above all when the dreaded
orange flame from perforated fuel lines began to lick round the
engine cowling – when the pilot had only a few minutes,
perhaps only a few seconds, to put his aircraft on the ground,
then all depended on his individual skill.

Anti-aircraft fire (*flak* in the Second World War) was known
as 'Archie', from a famous pre-war music hall song, regardless
of whether the shell-bursts were Allied or hostile. Without
radio-communication or ground control, searching pilots used
the clusters of AA shell-bursts as a location for homing on to
hostile aircraft. The Allied shells (British 3 in., or French
75 mm.) had a white smoke. The German was black cordite
and gave off an unpleasant, toxic smell that lingered even at
altitude in still air long after the fighting had passed over, so
that returning pilots would sometimes traverse a belt of this
vapour and look uneasily round the sky, banking their wings
to one side and another in a conditioned reflex.

At dawn, when the first patrols were flown and the sky was
a pale hemisphere of cinnamon or grey, it was impossible to
detect aircraft below you against the black carpet of the land.

But this safety at low altitudes was ephemeral, for with every minute that passed the air lightened and with it grew the risk that the patrolling scouts would be spotted before they could reach their combat altitude. And so the first minutes of the dawn were spent in climbing, climbing; only the pin-point clusters of orange fire that showed Archie bursting around some early spotter plane, could make it worth the hazard of a diversion.

German anti-aircraft guns.

This is the worst moment of the day. You don't usually sleep very well if you are down for a Dawn Patrol. The batman calls at 4.30 a.m. with cocoa and biscuits. I am always wide awake then. When it actually comes to the point – warming up, take-off, getting into formation and so on – you find yourself doing these things automatically. But then, when you see Archie below! It looks much worse in the dark, you can see the flames and this reminds you . . .

CHAPTER FOUR

Death

There were few flyers with any experience of air fighting who were not obsessed to some degree, though usually secretly, with the thought of being shot down in flames.*

Arthur Gould Lee

This was the paramount horror, the recurring nightmare, the insistent spectre that penetrated sleep and caused men to lie awake for hours before the dawn. No one who had flown in combat could have failed to see that terrible sight, an aircraft spiralling downwards in the black smoke of a gasoline fire. And it was only a matter of time before they saw one close enough to notice the last frenzies of the crew. Some would try to beat out the flames with their hands, others stood up and screamed curses, others would jump and fall, arms outstretched, clothing alight, from seven thousand feet. Still others (Bert Hall and James McCudden among them) carried a pistol, nominally for self-defence 'in case of forced landing in enemy territory'. It had only six rounds and only one purpose. Just a very few had the cool nerves and the flying skill to retain control of the aeroplane, to try to handle it down, or deliberately go into a stall to extinguish the flames with the back draught, although many perished in turning to this last resort. Richthofen's own combat log shows that out of eighty victories, fifty-four were *gebrannt* (burned).

On either side the pilots' allegorical names for gasoline – Infernal Liquid, The Hell-brew, Orange Death, Witches Water – underlined and perpetuated this phobia. Even after the ignition had been switched off the peril remained. The airscrew would continue to rotate with its own inertia and the force of the wind: it was locked in direct drive to the magneto which continued to emit sparks and these would ignite any fuel or vapour from broken feed pipes.

Sometimes, where serious engine damage had resulted in

* So wrote one of the survivors, Arthur Gould Lee, who subsequently rose to the rank of Air Vice Marshal – yet it took thirty years before he could bring himself to commit this view to paper. So deep-seated was the obsession that no mention of it can be found in any of the contemporary published accounts (although privately, in diaries and letters, it is found in profusion).

total seizure, the magneto stopped. Or for some other miraculous reason there would be no outbreak. But even in these cases pilots could have their nerve shattered, and perhaps lose their reason altogether during the long ordeal of bringing a damaged aircraft into land with their clothing soaked in gasoline. On nearly every aircraft the fuel tank was mounted in the nose as close to the engine as possible so as to simplify the feed and pump. This meant that the draught from the airscrew

Burning Farman crashing to the ground having been successfully attacked by German planes.

or, even if the airscrew had stopped, from forward flight, blew flames back into the pilot's face.

In the gunnery observation balloons where the crew hung with their headphones and binoculars, tethered by a wire rope, parachutes were issued. And many gunnery officers had made three or four jumps in escaping certain death by burning. The question of issuing parachutes to the pilots of the RFC was raised at staff level several times during 1916 and 1917, but the general view was that '. . . possession of a parachute might impair a pilot's nerve when in difficulties so that he would make improper use of his parachute.'

The Superintendent at Farnborough had made a number of

British aeroplane brought down in flames at Passchendaele in 1917.

experiments with parachutes and dummies, but when Major-General Sir David Henderson, GOC of the RFC, was minuted as to whether he wished the experiments to continue, he scrawled on the text in his own hand, 'No, certainly not!' General R. M. Groves committed himself to the view '. . . that smashed aircraft generally fall with such velocity that there would hardly be time to think about the parachute.'

Death lingered in the sky even as it does on land. There is no such thing as 'instantly'. One hundred and sixty pounds of flesh and blood, a complete nervous system, brain, heart, lungs, kidneys: heart pumping seventy-two times a minute (or more likely 125 in the stress and terror of combat), all these things do not surrender life however grievously stricken without a struggle. Only very occasionally when the first cluster of bullets smashed the pilot's skull did he pass into the Beyond without an ageless and agonized period of resistance. Sometimes, more than half the time, it was against the flames. At others, terrible pain and numbness, recurrent nausea and fainting in a cockpit where the blood sluiced audibly as the aircraft rolled from side to side. Some men went to their deaths unharmed in a stricken aeroplane that could no longer answer to the controls but dived or yawed, or spun, or slipped and fell with long deliberation like an autumn leaf before finally breaking against the solidity of earth and stone.

For most pilots with minimal imagination their first sight of a death in combat was traumatic. Repeated in close succession it led to nightmares, depression, withdrawal – symptoms that were ignored by a medical service that had no psychiatric branch. Still deeper was the impression made by the first direct 'kill'. One pilot wrote the whole account to his fiancée on the same evening:

I got my first Hun today! At last! . . .

Coming back, the formation split up and we made our separate ways. It was a lovely evening, very clear, with a pale blue sky, and I thought it was too nice to go straight back, I'd have another look at that incredible morass east of Ypres. I was half sliding down, northwards, just this side of the Hun balloon lines when I saw an RE 8 approaching on my left front, about 500 feet below. And tracers were spitting out from the observer's gun.

It was then that I realized that he was being followed and attacked by an Albatros V-Strutter from 150 yards' range, also firing short bursts. Before I could react, the Hun ceased firing, and turned east. I assumed he'd broken off because he'd spotted me. The RE whizzed past below, the observer waved, and the Albatros continued on a level course eastwards.

I dropped into a wide sweeping curve that brought me dead

Lieutenant-Colonel Audain, wearing a parachute harness, about to ascend in an observation balloon. The High Command refused to allow pilots to wear parachutes, justifying this action with the claim that it might 'impair a pilot's nerve'.

The parachute of an officer descending from an observation balloon caught in the branches of a tree.

Crashed BE 2C.

behind the Hun, and 200 feet above him. He was still flying level, due east, but not going flat out. It seemed incredible that he hadn't seen me when he turned aside from the RE. It looked so easy I suspected a trap, and searched carefully around, but there was no other machine in sight.

I came down closer and closer, holding my fire. My heart was pounding, and I was trembling uncontrollably, but my mind was calm and collected. I closed to ten yards, edged out of his slip-stream, drew nearer still until I saw that if I wasn't careful I'd hit his rudder. His machine was green and grey, and looked very spick and span. He had a dark brown flying helmet, with a white goggles-strap round the back of his head.

I aimed carefully through the Aldis between his shoulders just below where they showed above the fairing. It was impossible to miss. I gently pressed the trigger, and at the very first shots his head jerked back, and immediately the plane reared up vertically. He must have clutched the joy-stick right back as he was hit. I followed upwards, still firing, until in two or three seconds he stalled and fell over to the left, and I had to slew sharply aside to avoid being hit. He didn't spin, but dropped into a near-vertical engine-on dive.

I went after him, throttle wide open, firing in long bursts, but he gradually left me behind. I followed, still firing through the Aldis, until he was 300 yards distant, then I stopped, there was no point in pumping any more lead into him. But I stayed in the dive and saw that he didn't pull out . . .

A few pilots lived to tell the tale of that fatal moment in a dog fight when the engine stopped.

Instantly there was silence. And for a few seconds this silence (as it seemed by contrast with what had preceded it) would be total. Then, first to intrude because it was nearest, the song and moaning of the wires in the rigging. And hard on its heels the exhausts of other engines: the rattle, on every side, of other guns.

To the crew of this one aircraft life and death would be in perfect equilibrium. If it was only the engine that had suffered, and if it had given out on account of some mechanical failure of its own their chances were good. Given reasonable height and cool handling, the aeroplane could glide on to friendly territory. At worst its crew would finish as prisoners of war.

Even if they were seen by an enemy and their plight detected, there was a convention on both sides that persisted at least until 1918 that 'dead-stick' aeroplanes were left to their fate. Yet was not this convention honoured many times in the breach? The novices, the vindictive, the cold-blooded, those eager to add cheaply to their score, could not resist the easy and defenceless target which was offered to them.

On return there would be no inquiry concerning those who were missing once the de-briefing was over. The subject was not referred to. The policy of Trenchard, the RFC's commander in France for 1915–17, of 'no empty chairs', kept the messes full, even though it meant offering up the inexperienced and the partly trained as human sacrifices. It was the death of the wounded, those who had made it back over the line, in field hospitals and dressing stations, that made the biggest impact, and for that reason many pilots were reluctant to visit the hospitals even when their closest friends were detained there. Everyone dreaded the funerals, the silent crowd around an earth grave in some humble corner of a French village churchyard, marked by the white painted crossed blades of a shattered airscrew.

There is no better description of the agonizing spectacle that death provided and the protective callousness which it produced, than Cecil Lewis' account of Lieutenant Roberts' crash after his tail was damaged:

Roberts was a crack pilot, and if human skill could have got that machine out, he would have done it. His elevators and ailerons were still intact, and by shutting off his engine he almost managed to avert disaster – but not quite.

He could not stop the machine spinning: but he could stop it going into a vertical diving spin. He tried every combination of elevator and bank. No good. The machine went on slowly spinning, round, and round, and round, all the way down from eight thousand feet to the ground. It took about five minutes. He and his observer were sitting there, waiting for death, for that time.

The machine fell just this side of the lines. They say a man in the trenches heard shouts, as it might have been for help, come from the machine just before it struck the ground and smashed to a pile of wreckage.

The observer was killed, for the fuselage broke in half: but Roberts escaped. He was badly smashed up, but breathing. They got him on to a stretcher and sent him down to hospital. He had been out all through the Somme battle without leave, his nerves were right on the edge, and we heard, with what truth I never knew, that this fearful experience put him out of his mind. As far as we were concerned he was gone – the dead or wounded never came back to us – and in the swiftly changing pattern of the days we forgot him.

Part Three

The Killing Time

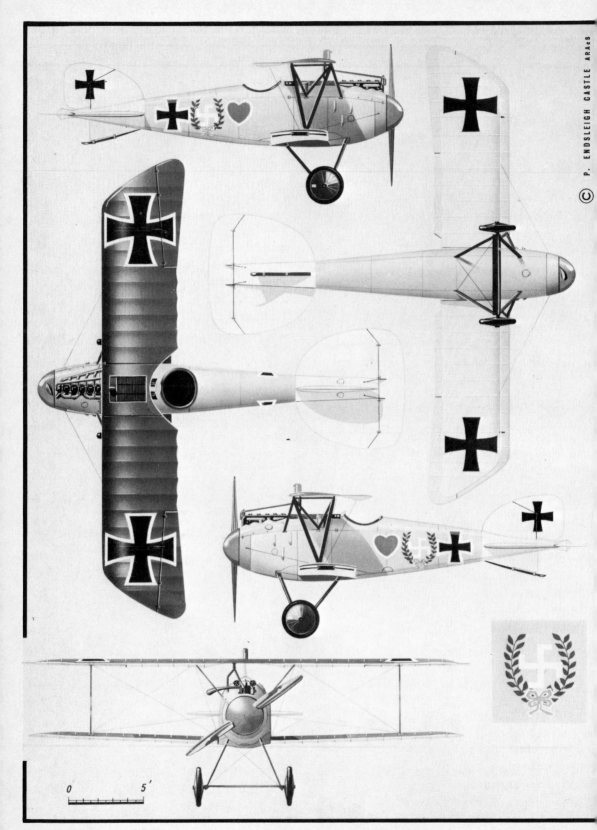

© P. ENDSLEIGH CASTLE ARAes

Albatros D III

Background 1917

By the beginning of 1917, the German Air Force had without a shadow of doubt gained the ascendancy over the Allies in the air over the Western Front. This had started with the introduction of the Albatros D I and II in the previous year. These fighters, though marginally superior to contemporary Allied types in performance, had a clear advantage in firepower, being equipped with two belt-fed and synchronized machine-guns to the Allied types' single belt- or drum-fed type. Now the Germans were introducing their latest fighter, the Albatros D III. This was a development of the earlier Albatri (as machines of this marque were known generically in the RFC), but was fitted with an up-rated engine and a new form of wing, derived from that of the French Nieuport, which had achieved such marked success against German machines in the previous year.

This new wing planform was the sesquiplane type, in which the lower wing is shorter in span than the upper and considerably narrower in chord. The two wings are connected to each other by a pair of V-shaped struts, which led to the RFC's nickname for the D III, and its later development the D V and Va, as the 'Vee-strutter'. The advantages inherent in this planform, increased manœuvrability and a much better downward view for the pilot, were to a certain extent offset by its one major disadvantage, the structural weakness of the lower wing. This was caused by its narrowness, which meant that the structure had to be built up around a single spar, which in turn left the wing weak in torsion. There were several instances of Vee-strutters developing 'flutter' in their lower wings and having them break off, normally with fatal consequences. Despite this, however, the Albatros was in every way superior to Allied types at the outset of 1917.

The German Jastas, which in April numbered thirty-seven, as already mentioned, were almost invariably passive in their defence of the skies over the Western Front, very seldom crossing over to the west of the lines. This, though it lost them the strategic initiative in the air, gave them a decided tactical advantage. For with these tactics they were able to climb into the sun over their own lines and wait, in numbers of considerable superiority, for the inevitable Allied reconnaisance and artillery observation machines that would cross the lines. Their task was made all the easier by the

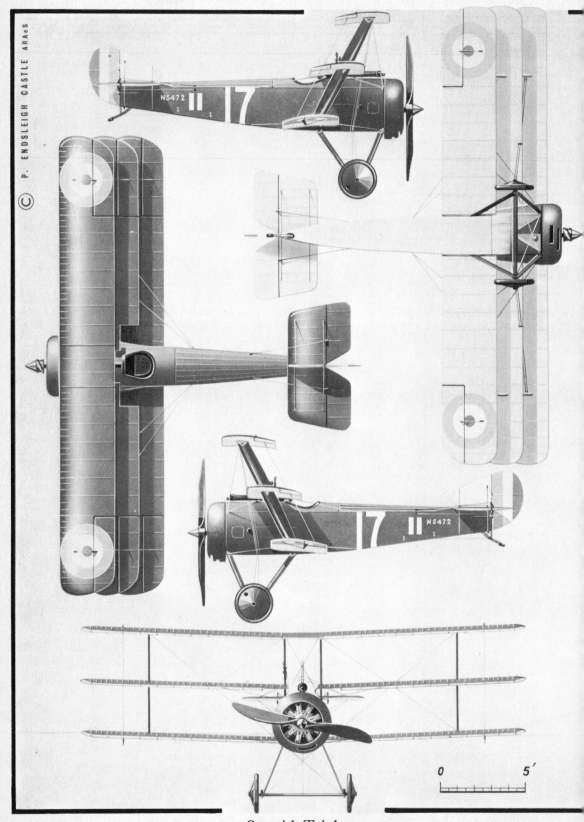

© P. ENDSLEIGH CASTLE ARAeS

Sopwith Triplane

two-seaters in use with the Allies; the old Moranes and the new Sopwith $1\frac{1}{2}$-Strutters just coming into service with the French Air Force, and the $1\frac{1}{2}$-Strutters, BE 2s, and RE 8s of the RFC.

April 1917 was set for the first big Allied offensive of the year, when the British were to launch a large scale offensive around Arras to draw German reserves away from the sector slightly to the south, where the French were to launch yet another offensive intended to drive the Germans out of the war. When it started, the French, under General Robert George Nivelle, suffered enormous reverses and casualties, which so shattered the morale of the French army, still suffering as it was from the titanic struggle for Verdun in the previous year, that widespread mutinies occurred, and the army ceased to be able to take part in any major offensive action for over a year. The British offensive at Arras, though successful on the ground, albeit with herculean casualties, was a disaster in the air.

The RFC was decimated. Casualties were something in the order of one third. These were the highest losses suffered by the RFC in the course of the whole war, and Trenchard received considerable criticism for insisting that the RFC continue to fly offensive patrols in inferior aircraft against an enemy admirably prepared to take advantage of such a situation. The RFC suffered losses, particularly in aircrew, that were to take more than a year to rectify. But it was not the numbers that were the most important loss, tragic as they were, but the skill and experience of the pilots and gunners who had learnt how to cope with the new conditions of aerial warfare in the second half of 1916. These were lost in great numbers, and the long-term effects included the continued alarmingly high rate of casualties among the inexperienced pilots who had to be posted straight from flying school to a front line squadron, even after the Battle of Arras had ended. The life expectancy of a subaltern, from the time of his posting to a front line squadron, varied from eleven days to three weeks. The Allies suffered grievous losses, and it was the German Air Force's high summer.

During April, the Allies' only successful aircraft had been the new fighter from the Sopwith stable, the Triplane. Still underarmed by German standards, it was able to hold its own by virtue of its phenomenal rate of climb and considerable agility, unmatched by anything the German could put up against it. The Triplane was operated only by the RNAS units serving on the Channel coast around Dunkirk, although it had been intended that the RFC receive the type. This did not occur, however, as it had been agreed between the Admiralty and the War Office in July 1916 that the RNAS should receive the 'Tripehound', as it was nicknamed, which was then under development for the RFC, in exchange for the Spad VIIs which the RNAS agreed to transfer to the RFC

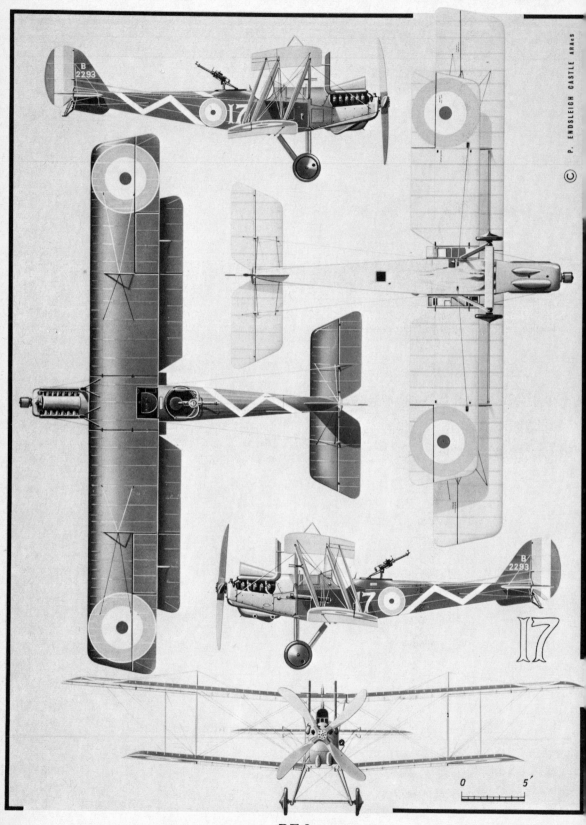

P. ENDSLEIGH CASTLE ARAeS

©

RE 8

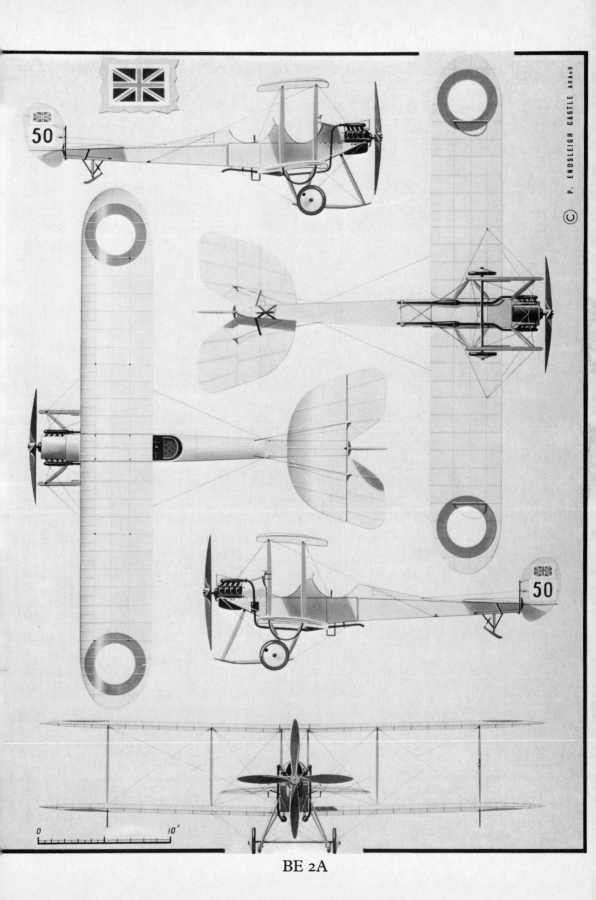

© P. ENDSLEIGH CASTLE ARAeS

50

50

0   10'

BE 2A

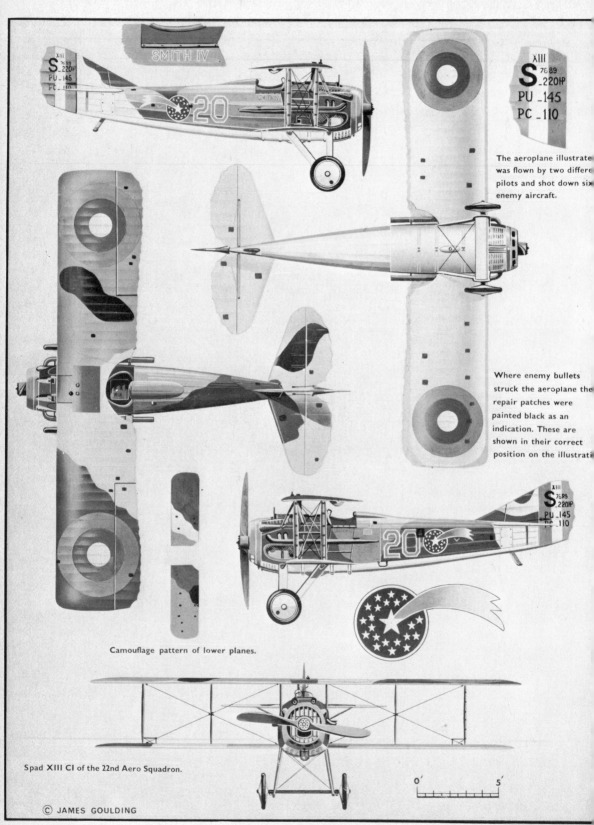

SMITH IV

XIII
S 7689
S .220 HP
PU .145
PC .110

The aeroplane illustrated
was flown by two different
pilots and shot down six
enemy aircraft.

Where enemy bullets
struck the aeroplane the
repair patches were
painted black as an
indication. These are
shown in their correct
position on the illustration

Camouflage pattern of lower planes.

Spad XIII CI of the 22nd Aero Squadron.

0'   5'

© JAMES GOULDING

Spad XIII

during the crucial days of the Battle of the Somme. In the crisis of the Battle of Arras and Bloody April, the RFC requested that naval units equipped with the Triplane should be sent south to aid the sorely pressed RFC. The Admiralty sent No. 10 Squadron. The Triplane's success was immediate and considerable, a fact testified to by the number of triplane designs originated in Germany after the arrival of the Sopwith original, but it could not halt the slaughter of RFC machines and men. All it could do was point to better things in the future.

There was no let-up in the RFC's offensive tactics after the end of the Battle of Arras, though the scale was considerably diminished. During the breathing space so afforded, a new generation of Allied fighters, destined to overcome the dominance of the Albatros, appeared, taking over from the now badly outclassed Sopwith Pup, outnumbered Sopwith Triplane (only 140 were ever built) and outgunned Spad VII and Nieuport 17. The first of the new generation to arrive was the SE 5, designed by the Royal Aircraft Factory. This was a rugged, angular biplane, very fast, equipped with two machine-guns (though one of these was a Lewis gun mounted on the top wing rather than a second belt-fed weapon in the fuselage) and possessing a fair measure of the inherent stability to be found in all production RAF types. In the SE 5 and its successor, the up-engined SE 5A, this inheritance was not a drawback, however, but a positive advantage, as it made the SE 5 one of the best gun platforms (which is really all a fighter is) of the war. The other Allied fighter to enter service at about the same time was the French Spad XIII, an up-engined and up-gunned development of the Spad VII. In a way the fighters were similar, both possessing excellent performance, and having the same sort of angular lines and strength, but the Spad had the advantage in armament, with two Vickers guns in the fuselage.

Both had teething troubles when they entered service, and the SE 5 also suffered from wrong tactics in the hands of pilots who had before flown only light, sensitive, rotary-engined fighters. But once these initial difficulties had been overcome, the two machines proved to be amongst the best Allied fighters of the war, continuing in production right up to the end of hostilities.

The eclipse of the Albatros began with the arrival of the SE 5 in late April and of the Spad XIII in late May, and was made certain in July on the arrival of the first of the Allies' most successful fighter, the Sopwith Camel. Unlike its contemporaries the SE 5A and the Spad XIII, the Camel had a rotary engine, and had a distinct family likeness to the Pup. But its strength lay in an adequate performance, two Vickers guns and a superlative aerobatic capability, excelled possibly only by the Pup and the Fokker triplane, the Dr I. Although it was in the process of replacement by

© P. ENDSLEIGH CASTLE ARAeS

B
6234

B
6234

0   5′

Sopwith Camel

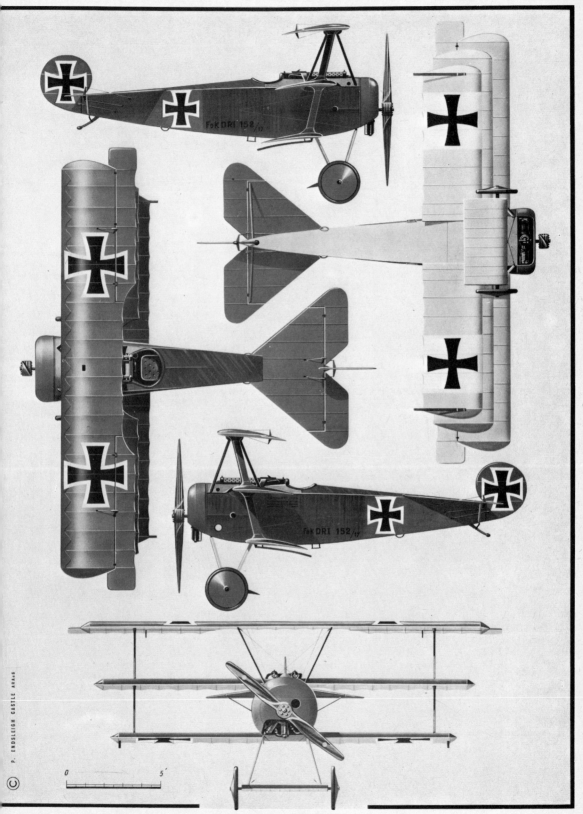

© P. ENDSLEIGH CASTLE ARAGS

0   5'

Fokker Dr I

the Sopwith Snipe and Dolphin in the closing months of the war, the Camel remains the classic rotary-engined fighter of the First World War.

The Germans, confident of continued success with the Albatros D III after April, failed to press on with the planning of a successor, so that when the Albatros supremacy began to crumble in face of the Spad XIII and SE 5A, they had to have recourse to a hurried programme to update the D III. This resulted in the introduction of the D V at about the time the Camel was making its début on the Allied side. But the improvements made in the Albatros in the way of streamlining and increased engine power were offset by the increase in weight, so that the later mark was no better than its predecessor. The only other German fighter to appear in any number at about this time was the Fokker Dr I triplane, which owed its inspiration to the Sopwith Triplane. The Dr I entered service in August 1917, during the period that the obsolescence of the Triplane had become embarrassing to the RNAS. Although its design was anachronistic in comparison with the Allied designs entering service in autumn 1917, it obtained considerable success as a result of its enormous manœuvrability, good firepower and the fact that it was issued only to the best of the German pilots, who enjoyed the advantage, conferred on them by their defensive tactics and the prevailing Westerly wind, of being able to fight over their own lines and glide towards their airfields with the aid of the wind if they received any damage.

Finally, as far as the aircraft themselves are concerned in 1917, one must take note of the arrival of the superb Bristol F 2A and B in the spring of 1917. With the introduction of this two-seater, the Allies at last had a reconnaissance and general purpose machine as good as, if not better than, anything the Germans had. As with the SE 5, its entry into front line service was not particularly auspicious, but soon its crews realized that although it was a two-seater it had the performance, firepower and manœuvrability to take on fighters at their own game. From then on, its success was assured, and it went down in history as the most versatile aircraft of the First World War.

In the field of tactics and organization also, 1917 proved to be the great turning point. The arrival of true fighters in 1916 had led to their introduction in small quantities initially, and this had resulted in the fighter pilot being for the most part a lone flyer, using stealth to stalk and dispatch his opponent. The tactical counter to this was the introduction of the Jasta, and the homogeneous fighter squadrons and Escadrilles de Chasse, and the year had ended with a presentiment of what was to come, as more and more units took to the skies to fight in formation. The reply to this first counter was thought of and put into practice first by the Germans. This was the Jagdgeschwader or fighter wing. The first

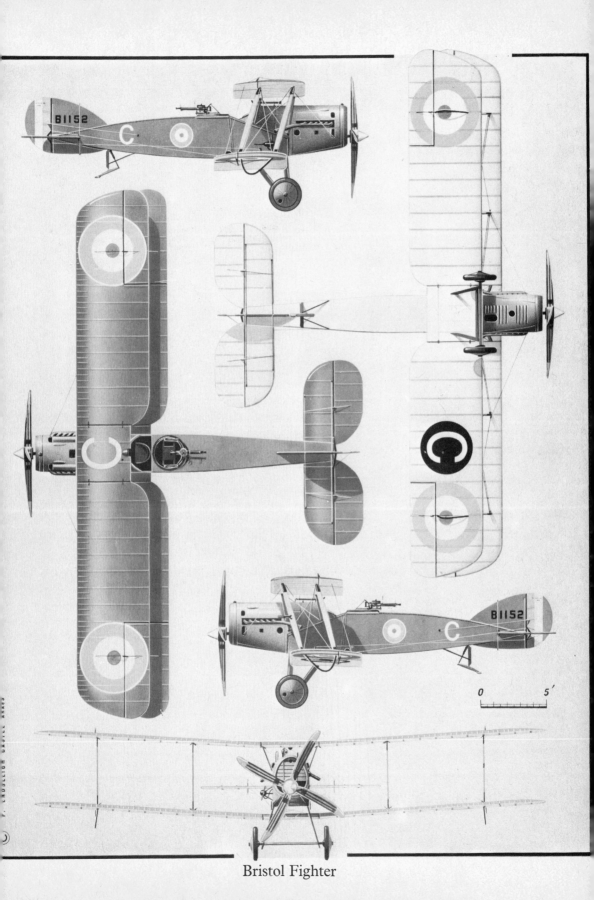

Bristol Fighter

of these, No. 1, was formed under Manfred von Richthofen's command on 26 July 1917. Basically it was an amalgam of Jastas *4, 6, 10 and 11, and was provided with many lorries and other mobile equipment, so that it could be shuttled up and down the line to provide air superiority wherever it might be needed at any particular moment. Thus the Germans, who by now could not hope to attain an overall air superiority, could gain a local and necessary one by the dispatch to that sector of a large and élite unit. The aircraft of such units were often painted in garish colours, since camouflage was unnecessary, as a means of recognition between members of the same unit, and led to the Allies dubbing the* Jagdgeschwader *'Flying Circuses'. The only other* Jagdgeschwader, *Nos. 2, 3 and 4 were all formed in 1918. The other new type of German unit to be formed was the* Jagdgruppe *or fighter group, which was between the* Jasta *and* Geschwader *in size, usually made up of two or three* Jastas. *Twelve were formed eventually, but these were not permanent bodies, but rather* ad hoc *forces united for a special purpose. When that purpose had been fulfilled, the* Jagdgruppe *was disbanded.*

The British counterpart to the Jagdgeschwader *and* Jagdgruppe *was the Wing, which might contain anything up to five squadrons to deal with an emergency. The French, unlike the British, had élite units, such as* Les Cigognes *or* Les Sportifs, *and though these were composed of several smaller units, the various component parts did not often serve together. But in the event of an emergency, the* Escadrilles *could be called together to provide local air superiority. The system of calling together large numbers of aircraft under a unified control for a special purpose was still gathering momentum in 1917, and although a few large scale battles took place towards the end of the year, they were small in comparison with what 1918 was to bring. With a few extraordinary exceptions, however, the increasing systemization of aerial fighting had sounded the death knell of the individual ace, such as Albert Ball and Georges Guynemer.*

The most important organizational change of the year was the decision by the British Government to set up the Royal Air Force, though this only came into being on 1 April 1918. The summer of 1917 had been marked by the periodic arrival of German bombers over the skies of southern England, and such was the political and popular furore, demanding protection for Britain and retribution on the Germans, that the government had set up a committee under General Jan Christian Smuts, the South African statesman and soldier, to investigate means of satisfying both these demands. In the short term, two of the RFC's best squadrons were brought back from France (where they were sadly missed) to provide a token defence. In the long term, the committee found that it would be best to amalgamate the RFC and RNAS, whose equipment requirements had led to a wholly uneconomical priorities system in the British aircraft manufacturing trade, under a ministry independent of the War Office and the Admiralty. Such was the increase in production anticipated from this rationalization of resources (an expectation which proved entirely unjustified), that the committee also recommended that the new Royal Air Force, when it came into being, should set up a strategic bombing force along the lines of the French one that had been operating since 1915. This force, which became the Independent Air Force, Royal Air Force, finally comprised British, French, Italian and American squadrons. However, it was a year before these plans came to fruition.

With the American declaration of war on Germany on 6 April, both sides foresaw huge American reinforcements for the Allied war effort, and Germany instituted a major programme of rearmament to beat the Allies before the weight of American production and manpower could make itself felt.

As early as 3 June 1917 there was a conference attended by all senior officers of Kogenluft at which the situation was reviewed in the light not only of the mounting threat from the RFC but of the longer term menace (in fact considerably overrated) of American industry following the declaration of war by the United States. The aerial programme had also to fit in with the OHL (German Army High Command) strategy which was for a knockout blow on the Western Front in the spring of 1918 – this also being calculated on the necessity of striking before the American scale of reinforcement became too great.

The plan, known as the Amerika-Programm, had to be complete in all its aspects by 1 March 1918 and provided for: 1. Enlargement of the thirteen existing flying training schools; 2. Formation of a second Jasta training school; 3. Aircraft production to be doubled to 2,000 per month; 4. Engine production to be increased from 1,250 to 2,500 per month; 5. The reallocation of 7,000 skilled workers from other branches of the armed forces; 6. Machine-gun production to be increased to 1,500 per month; 7. Aviation fuel production to be raised from 6,000 to 12,000 tons per month. There were a number of other provisions relating to the necessary machine tools and raw materials, especially aluminium.

CHAPTER FIVE

Aces

One must first overcome the
inner *schweinehund*

Manfred von Richthofen

A great divide separated the novice from the experienced. It was a gulf that separates those who are going to die from those who may survive.

The new faces, nervous, enthusiastic, with their playing-field grins, were ignored, or almost. They arrived, unloaded their kit; often the previous occupant's effects and possessions were still strewn about. They had the worst tents, the surliest batmen. It was recognized that their stay would be only temporary. In 1917 the life expectancy of a subaltern in the RFC from posting until death was eleven days.

Cowardice was a deadly sin. The veto was absolute. In discussion fear was masked by bravado – 'Chaps, here goes!' Only in the privacy of diaries, very occasionally in letters to relatives, do these forebodings emerge:

There have been two changes in the bunk next to me since April Fool's Day (last week!) I wouldn't sleep in it for all the tea in China.

Poor old B – caught it yesterday, down in flames over Menin. He had been acting strange for the last few days, wandering about speaking to himself.

From a diary:
Turned back again today with mag failure (ha ha). In a blue funk in case Sgt. Mellish 'told' on me. But he dutifully took the whole thing to bits and reassembled it and kept mum.

Garett has been moved to a room of his own. He had been kicking up such a shindig in the night with his dreams of burning, spinning and such like that we three complained and got him billetted solo.

Squadrons varied in their attitude to new-comers. Some commanders took great care to nurture their replacements and avoid exposing them to serious risks in their first days. They were taken on personally conducted tours of the battle area,

Opposite Manfred von Richthofen with members of *Jasta 11* in 1917: (from left to right) Sebastian Festner, Emil Schaefer, Lothar von Richthofen (Manfred's brother) and Kurt Wolff.

Parade of RFC
recruits still in their
civilian clothes.
Sometimes new
arrivals were broken in
gently, but more
frequently they were
given little help and
left to fend for
themselves by the
more experienced
pilots.

Opposite Oswald
Boelcke; his skill lay
not only in his
evaluation of aircraft
and application of
combat tactics, but in
his far-sighted ideas
on fighter unit
organization. At his
suggestion the new
units known as
Jagdstaffeln were
formed with Boelcke
leading *Jasta 2*,
renamed after his
death as *Jasta Boelcke*.

were changed round with experienced crew members (new
pilot with experienced observer and vice versa) and were
positioned second and third in the standard tactical formation,
known as the Vee, on offensive patrols so that they could take
their cue from the leader (for one of the beginners' most
serious defects was his inability to see the enemy).

But in other units they were left to fend for themselves.
Experienced flyers strongly disliked the idea of putting themselves at risk by taking up a raw observer. Hardened observers
who had survived many critical battles, and whose nerves
cannot have gone unaffected, refused to put their fate in the
hands of a young pilot fresh from England whose combat
ability was completely untried. There were many bad instances
in that terrible spring of 1917 when new pilots flew at the tail
of the squadron because they were ordered there. At the first
sign of combat the hardened tip would break off hustling its
way down and home in the first hectic minutes of the dog fight
and leaving the apprentices to be cut up by the enemy.
'Missing' was a more comfortable definition of a casualty than
'seen to go down in flames'.

Some, very few, could make the transition from novice to
ace. Oswald Boelcke, one of the first and father of fighter
tactics and organization had achieved this and, as he was much
photographed, it is possible to trace in his features the scars of
that experience. First the early pictures; shaven head, pene-
trating blue eyes, the confidence and *tenu* of a chivalrous young
Prussian. But then, frighteningly soon, the shadows form; the
eyes enlarge, but hollow in their sockets. The flesh falls away
from neck and hand and wrist, accentuating the line of bone and

sinew. In group pictures those round him are evidently pleased to be in his company and reflect his glory, some are even smiling. But never Boelcke. Already he has seen too many planes burning. It was the practice of the Germans to visit the site of their opponent's crash in order to confirm their combat report and only the final question concerned Boelcke – would his own death be *'fercht oder getrocknet'* (literally 'wet or dry' i.e. burned or mutilated to death). It was *'fercht'* following a collision in combat on 28 October 1916.

This same expression can be seen in the eyes of Georges Guynemer, the French ace of *Les Cigognes*, France's élite fighter unit. There is a picture of him taken towards the end of his life, showing a man razor thin, hollow-eyed, bedecked with medals and honours, staring not at, but beyond the photographer, with eyes de-focused, as if in a trance.

Guynemer had been right through the battle of Verdun where the *Cigognes* were based at Nancy. In June of 1917 when he was appointed an officer of the Legion of Honour, his score of kills stood at forty-five. Now he had to bring the *Cigognes* north to help the RFC clear the unfamiliar skies of Flanders while first the Battle of Messines and then of Passchendaele were fought out below. He was granted three precious days leave. His father begged him to retire and take a position as an instructor and technical adviser. The old man was shocked by his son's appearance and knew, intuitively, that if Guynemer returned to combat, he would never see him again. But Guynemer was a victim of his own publicity machine. Although half-persuaded, he claimed that he could not retire from combat for fear of *what would be said*. *'On dira'*, he told his father, 'that I have ceased to fight because I have won all the awards.' In vain his father argued that he could always return, that he would be stronger and more ardent and that when he did so everyone would understand. In vain he reminded his son of all the crashes, the forced landings and wounds which he had sustained and how providence could not look after him forever. 'There is a limit to human strength', Guynemer's father told him. But this, the philosophy of age and experience, was unacceptable. Before he went back to the front, Guynemer told his father, 'Indeed there is a limit. But it is only there to be excelled. If one has not given everything, one has given nothing.'

When Guynemer arrived at St Pol-sur-mer where the *Cigognes* were now based, he learned that one of his closest friends, Capitaine A. Heurtaux had been seriously wounded the day before. His own favourite Spad was unserviceable (it had been brought to St Pol from Nancy by an inexperienced pilot when Guynemer was on leave). Incredibly, Guynemer

Above Alfred Heurtaux, a famous member of the *Cigognes* group and a close friend of Georges Guynemer. He scored twenty-one victories until a serious wound in September 1917 made him unable to fly again during the war.

Opposite Georges Guynemer, bedecked with medals, shortly before his death in September 1917.

Felix Brocard, the commanding officer of the famous *Cigognes* group.

was forced to fly his sorties in second-rate aircraft – those awaiting replacement pilots or, worse still, in the queue for workshop attention. On one day three different aeroplanes had engine or structural failure while he was flying them; in each case he brought off a forced landing. A less skilful pilot would have been killed. Twice his guns had jammed in combat. For four consecutive days he flew five patrols of two and a half hours each, but without scoring a victory. Guynemer was now fast becoming a victim of a paranoiac condition. At night he could not sleep but would pace the floor of his bedroom, talking to himself, or go and rouse his mechanics to swing the prop of his aircraft and run up the engine under the light of the moon. He believed that there was a whispering about him in the mess, that he was deliberately avoiding combat because of his inferiority at the controls of worn out aeroplanes . . . 'such as the ordinary pilot has to fly'.

Word got back to Paris and two emissaries were dispatched to investigate. Capitaine Felix Brocard, the *Cigognes*' Commanding Officer, and Commandant Jean du Peuty, commander of the French Air Force Aviation Staff at GWL (the French General Headquarters), arrived at St Pol at nine o'clock on the morning of 11 September. The sky was overcast and a light drizzle was falling. All the *Cigognes* were grounded with the exception of Guynemer and a *sous-lieutenant*, Benjamen Bozon-Verduraz, whom Guynemer had ordered to accompany him on an interception flight which had taken off at 8.30 a.m.

While the delegation from the Air Ministry waited impatiently at St Pol, Guynemer and Bozon had located an enemy two-seater over Poelcapelle and staged a conventional three o'clock and six o'clock attack (one coming in from the quarter and one from the rear). But it was a trap. Three Albatri escorting the two-seater behind and 3,000 feet above it, dived on the two Spads. Bozon saw them in time and turned to attack head-on, escaping in the mêlée. But Guynemer was never seen again. A few days later the Germans announced he had been shot down by a Leutnant Kurt Wissemann. No trace of Guynemer's body or aircraft was ever found. The very special Spad which du Peuty had had delivered that day from the factory at Buc was already second-hand.

With the possible exception of Manfred von Richthofen, none of the aces preserved their initial *sang froid*. Richthofen was totally cold-blooded, incapable of any close personal relationship, and his very aloofness gave him a special strength and heightened the devotion which his colleagues and subordinates paid him. He never relaxed, seldom smiled, disapproved of any

Manfred von Richthofen with his dog Moritz. He once wrote, 'The most beautiful thing in all creation is my Danish Hound, Moritz'.

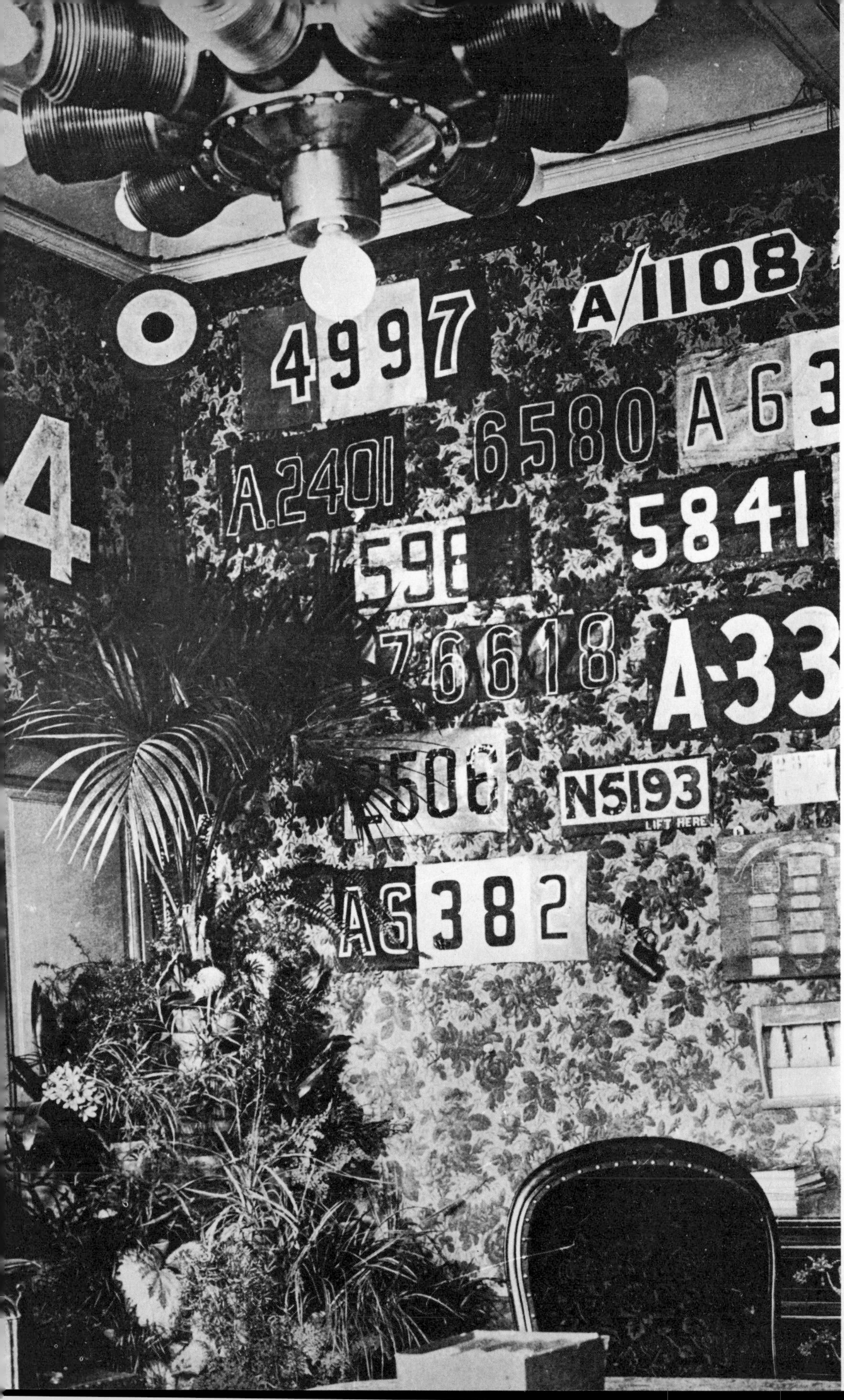
A/1108
4997
6580
A.2401
5841
76618
N5193
LIFT HERE
A6382

slackening of discipline or protocol. He had no intimate friends – although there were many who idolized him without their affection being returned. 'The most beautiful thing in all creation is my Danish Hound, Moritz', wrote Richthofen. Moritz slept on Richthofen's bed, and even flew on occasion although he must have weighed over a hundred pounds. On these flights Richthofen said that Moritz '. . . quite enjoyed himself and looked about intelligently'.

Opposite Richthofen's room decorated with serial numbers cut from the wreckage of aircraft that he had shot down.

But with this one exception Richthofen had no weaknesses. From his earliest youth he had found satisfaction only in killing things. He was a crack shot and kept the *Jasta* in game wherever they were stationed. A Prussian by birth, he had served with the Uhlans at the outbreak of war, transferred to the air service and flown as an observer, serving for several months under a mad consumptive pilot called Zeuner, who wanted to die and used to close the range to an impossibly dangerous proximity in combat. Richthofen's nerve held and after his experiences with Zeuner, nothing could ever have seemed quite as bad. He retained his cavalry breeches and always wore them with boots and a fur cap with ear flaps and a thin leather, hip-length jacket, belted and with a wide fur collar. After his victory over Lanoe Hawker, Richthofen adopted the practice of bringing back trophies from every aeroplane that he had shot down, just as formerly he had filled his mother's house with tusks and heads and antlers.

All the aces were kept, or kept themselves, in the firing line far too long (indeed Richthofen's own equanimity was undoubtedly helped as much by his frequent lay-offs as by his mastery of 'the inner *schweinehund*'). All could count and see how, statistically, their own death was a measurable happening. Superstition was intense and widespread. No pilot would go into a dive after his enemy without touching wood or some private talisman. Each narrow escape would be attributed to a particular piece of luck or propitiation of the fates, just as friends and colleagues who had suffered death from chance shots or aircraft breaking up were remembered on reflection to have flouted the *mores* of superstition.

Once *Jasta 11* suffered a particularly unnerving experience. On 17 September 1916, a BE 2C emerged from a cloud bank and flew straight into their formation. The *Jasta* broke up and took it in turn to attack the lumbering two-seater, whose crew made no effort to defend themselves, each pilot filling it with lead. The German pilots closed the range shorter and shorter, firing until their guns jammed. Pieces flew off the BE 2C, but it continued to fly a level course due east, finally disappearing into a towering bank of *alto cumulus*.

That evening the curious incident was the subject of

Members of *Jasta II*
in March 1917: (seated
in aircraft) Manfred
von Richthofen;
(seated on wing) Emil
Schaeffer; (standing
from left to right)
unknown, Hintsch,
Sebastian Festner,
Kurt Wolff, Simon,
Otto Brauneck;
(kneeling) Esser,
Kreft; (seated in
front) Lothar von
Richthofen.

Opposite Albert Ball;
eager and intense, he
was the epitome of the
young ex-public
school airman, a
striking contrast to
the tough pilots of
Jasta II

excitable discussion, when the news came through that the BE 2C had made a perfect landing in a field thirty miles inside the German lines. The petrol tank was bone dry and both members of the crew were dead with over fifty bullets in their bodies. A report from another *Jasta* indicated that the BE 2C had been attacked and damaged (but not seen to crash) some minutes before it had flown through Richthofen's formation. One of the Circus has described how: 'there was a distinct feeling of uneasiness at the news; there was something eerie about shooting at a crew of dead men. Was there an omen in the way they had ignored our bullets?'

But Richthofen was equal to the situation. At the end of the meal he hammered on the table and called for a toast:

A glorious death! Fight on and fly on to the last drop of blood and the last drop of petrol – to the last beat of the heart and the last kick of the motor; a death for a knight – a toast for his fellows, friend and foe.

As the aces looked back over their own escapes and ordeals – particularly when they had suffered wounding and later

returned to active duty – deep neuroses began to build up, their effect compounded by reflective guilt concerning all those pilots whom they had burned or shot, and a dark certainty that retribution awaited them.

One of his colleagues has described the nightly ordeal of Read Chambers, an American ace who had been in continuous combat for three months. He was:

. . . tormented by a nightmare: a face. The face would appear vague and distant, and would slowly come nearer until it seemed as if the face and Chambers were literally nose to nose, staring at each other. That's all, just staring. Then Chambers would wake up, his sleep spoiled. Who was it? Chambers was not superstitious, but it was a torment not to know to whom this disembodied face belonged. Was it a man he had killed? Or was it the man waiting for him in the sun?

Some of the aces, men like Albert Ball or Oswald Boelcke, did indeed start as carefree personifications of their country's youth. Their metamorphosis was a matter of weeks and months. But in others the death-wish was latent from the start. A miserable childhood, a lonely and introspective life, the handicaps of physical frailty or poor health, found release in the endless vista of the skies and the private trial of individual combat. Raoul Lufbery never saw his mother. His father deserted the home when the little boy was six years old. Bullied and neglected by relatives and neighbours, Lufbery focused all his love and ambition on the absent figure of his father and by the age of nineteen had saved enough money to attempt the journey to the United States to try and find him. Lufbery did not have enough money to cross the Atlantic from France and his attempt to stow away was discovered and brutally punished. He turned direction and made his way around the Mediterranean down through the Balkans and across Turkey with groups of itinerant labourers and vagrants, crossing North Africa in Arab caravans and finally taking a tramp steamer from Casablanca. Lufbery arrived in New York on the very day that his father, who had now become prosperous, sailed for Europe with the intention of finding his only son – and the two never met again. In despair the young Lufbery continued round the world, eking out a living wherever he could. He did a spell as a soldier of fortune in Indo-China and then met up with one of the earliest 'stunt' flyers and enlisted as his mechanic, teaching himself the theory of engineering. Next Lufbery taught himself to fly and finding himself back in France after the outbreak of war, he enlisted and sought death in the clouds. For a year he taught American volunteers until, almost accidentally, he was shot

down attacking a two-seater in low cloud over his own aero-drome, with his own score standing at seventeen kills.

Werner Voss, Richthofen's closest rival, stood in marked contrast to the Prussian nobleman. Of humble origin, he had enlisted in the Hussars when still under age. He had a passion for machinery and motorcycles, and graduated naturally into the Air Service, where he flew as an observer through the first months of the Battle of the Somme before being transferred to single-seaters in September. When he left his old unit, Voss recorded that not one single member of its strength who had been present on the day that he joined was still alive. His experience there left him with a lasting compassion for two-seater crews – the poor devils (*verachtliken*) as he called them – and he always made a practice of shooting down enemy two-seaters by a burst of fire into the engine-compartment so that the pilot might have a sporting chance of bringing the aeroplane down alive. Voss had crossed swords with James McCudden (the man who a year later was to lead the formation which killed him). McCudden was flying with

Raoul Lufbery in an American uniform wearing a major's insignia. He was one of the many members of the *Lafayette Escadrille* who transferred to the American Air Service when the USA entered the war.

'Mick' Mannock, the highest scorer of the British aces. Ruthless in battle, he was described as the outstanding fighter patrol leader of the war.

three others in DH 2s and Voss managed to escape by his superior aerobatics. At the time McCudden recorded the incident: '. . . a really clever Hun today. He knew his business alright, turning far tighter than we could manage. Last time he was within fifty feet of me and I swear he was grinning all over his face.'

Voss soon graduated to Albatri and became a flight leader in *Jasta 2*, Boelcke's old *Jasta* which had already lost two of its commanders. In January and February, Voss raised his score to twenty-two – uncomfortably close to that of von Richthofen (at that time twenty-seven). Then he was switched south to clear the skies of French aeroplanes during the Nivelle offensive of April 1917. Voss did not return to the British sector until July by which time the first of the SE 5s, Camels and Bristol Fighters were beginning to crack the domination of the Albatri. Voss was given command of *Jasta 10* and like Richthofen and the other leading aces, appropriated to himself one of the first Fokker triplanes to be delivered. It was painted light olive green with Maltese crosses on a white tail plane and a white ring on the fuselage. The wheel discs and wing undersurfaces were coloured light blue and the front of the nacelle housing the Oberursel rotary engine was painted to depict a terrifying grimace around the two eyes of the air intake, in the manner of a totem pole. Although he led *Jasta 10* with great success, Voss's preference was still for solitary patrols at dawn and dusk and, ultimately, it was on one of these that he met his death.

If one were to nominate the three primary aces of the Royal Flying Corps it would have to be Lanoe Hawker, Albert Ball and 'Mick' Mannock. There are many other claimants, certainly – A.P.F.Rhys-Davids, William Bishop, James McCudden, Raymond Collishaw – all made their contributions in their own individual terms and typified a whole strain of pilots that idolized them. But these three were archetypal. Hawker; distinguished, moustachioed, elderly by comparison with the fledglings that followed him; a crack-shot, a classic example of a type that the Great War was to extinguish forever – the chivalrous, Edwardian gentleman of private means. Mannock; Hawker's very opposite. Of humble birth, burning with social indignation, ruthless in battle, a man who had no time for the horseplay or posturings of the officers' mess, who refused to attend his enemies' funerals or drop wreaths or messages over enemy aerodromes, a man who jumped a German flying training school, killed the instructor and had no scruples about pursuing his five pupils in their unwieldy Aviatik trainers and setting light to them one by one. He was killed in 1918, with at least seventy-three victims to his credit, and the lasting reputation as the war's greatest patrol leader and mentor of novices.

And Ball; no hero of the First World War combines so strongly those national characteristics which Scott FitzGerald identified in *Tender is the Night* as the root cause of its incredible ferocity, of why '. . . it could only be fought once in five generations'.

Ball was a perfect public schoolboy. He had the enthusiasms and all the eager intelligence of that breed. But of course he had joined at eighteen; he had no experience of life, he had no outlet for his affections (he wrote only to his mother, thanking her for cake and provisions in much the same way as he must have done from school), he was in every sense immature. These are the ingredients of a perfect killer, where a smooth transition can be made between the motives that drive a boy to 'play hard' at school and then to 'fight hard' against the King's enemies.

At first Ball was attached to No. 13 Squadron and with them he flew many hundreds of hours on observation before the

Battle of the Somme in the elderly and vulnerable BE 2C. But in those days squadrons were not uniform in their equipment and Ball coveted and, whenever possible, showed his prowess in the little single-seater Bristol Scout that was attached to the squadron. He was transferred to No. 11, theoretically an exclusively fighter squadron which by good fortune was being re-equipped with French Nieuports. Ball quickly realized that the Nieuport had such a margin of superiority over all other aircraft at that time that he made a practice of taking on enormous formations of German aeroplanes single-handed, knowing that unless luck was against him he would be able to shoot down at least one German aeroplane while the enemy came to their senses, and thereafter the speed and manœuvrability of the Nieuport would allow him to escape. Throughout June and July 1916, Ball's score accumulated. Each time he sent a German down in flames he felt, as he put it in his letters '. . . utterly rotten'. But duty was inexorable. Many times his own aeroplane was riddled so badly by machine-gun fire that it had to be scrapped on return. Three times he crashed, once being saved only by a miracle. Statistically, Ball must have known that his life was coming to a close, and that same distant look which haunts the gaze of all those aces who allowed themselves to be photographed late in their career, can be discerned in the photographs of Ball. After his award of the MC and his fourth narrow escape, Ball's score stood at thirty-two enemy planes. He wrote to his mother: 'I just feel absolutely through, all in. I am going to ask them for a rest. I don't think they can refuse me, I have flown a patrol every day this year.'

Incredibly, the authorities did refuse this request. Worse, Ball was transferred back to No. 13 Squadron where he had to resume the most dangerous task of all, namely flying as a sitting target in BE 2C observer planes. His nerves at breaking point, Ball applied for a transfer back to his old squadron. '. . . that made you see sense, eh?' said his Corps Commander (who did not fly).

Ball remained in the line, and survived, for a further three months. Then providentially he was sent back to England, there being assigned to a training school and remaining until February of the following year, when he was appointed Flight Commander in the new, crack Squadron No. 56 that was being formed to take on Richthofen with the SE 5.

Opposite Hermann Goering; one of the best German fighters of the First World War, he lived to command the *Luftwaffe* in the Second World War and was second only to Hitler.

CHAPTER SIX

Circuses

I am a hunter. My brother, Lothar, is a butcher. When I have shot down an Englishman my hunting passion is satisfied for a quarter of an hour.

Manfred von Richthofen

It was a particularly unfortunate coincidence that the decline of the RAF from exhaustion in the Battle of the Somme co-incided with the arrival of the Albatros. Throughout the winter of 1916–17, their numbers multiplied at a frightening rate. After taking into account combat losses and wastage (accident damage, unserviceability) German operational strength, in Albatri alone, had risen from 7 in September, to 78 in November, 270 in January and 305 in March. By May of 1917, it was to stand at 434. A total of thirty-seven separate *Jastas* of fourteen aircraft each controlled through the *Flugmelde-dienst* or Flight Report Service which liaised by telephone, from the ground troops and observation through to the duty officer, at the *Jasta* airfields. In June of 1917, the principle of concentration was carried still further when the Germans began to amalgamate *Jastas* into *Jagdgeschwader* (*JG*). For example, *Jastas 4, 6, 10* and *11* were amalgamated into *JG 1* under Richthofen with instructions 'to attain air supremacy in sectors of the front as directed'.

Now the enemy had simultaneously attained superiority in equipment, in numbers (by virtue of his concentration), in skill (the *Jasta* pilots were all picked) and, resulting from these, in morale.

The brief period of superiority which the RFC had enjoyed during the early days of the Somme offensive – and which had been largely due to its enormous numerical preponderance and the DH 2 fighter, and to the dash and courage of a few picked groups, notably that led by Hawker – was gone. The skill and bravery of those experienced pilots were useless against the superior speed, armament and rate of climb of the Albatros. Only the Sopwith Triplane could give the Germans a fair fight. And the enemy always avoided the Triplane formations – which was not difficult as they were all grouped in the far North under RNAS command.

Opposite Albatros D IIIs of Richthofen's *Jasta II* at Douai in France just before the offensive of March 1917. Richthofen's plane is the second one from the front, without the Iron Cross on the tail.

One other aeroplane had a chance. The tiny Sopwith 'Pup' could still, on account of its light weight and perfect manœuvrability, get the better of the Albatros at extreme altitudes. Nos. 54 and 46 Squadrons had a song of their own sung to the tune of *We've Come up From Somerset*:

> Oh, we've come up from Fifty-four,
>   We're the Sopwith Pups, you know,
> And wherever you beastly Huns may be
>   The Sopwith Pups will go.
> And if you want a proper scrap,
>   Don't chase BEs any more,
> For we'll come up and do the job,
>   Because we're Fifty-four!

There, at 17,000 feet and over, the pilots gasped for lack of oxygen as they struggled with the controls. It was an unknown land whose towering banks of freezing cloud and bitter temperatures denied entry to any but the bravest in the winter months. The Pup took nearly an hour to climb to its maximum. During that period, or when descending, it was prey to the more powerful German single-seaters whose twin machine-guns had nearly three times of the rate of fire of the Pup's single Vickers.

A few minutes later, at 17,000, Scott dived on a group of five (Albatros) D–Vs about 1,000 feet below, and the eight of us might have knocked them into a cocked hat but for one small thing. Fourteen – yes, 14! – more Albatri rushed along and joined in. We learned the number afterwards from Armitage, whose engine cut out in a dive, and who watched them swooping on us as he glided westwards.

When we dived, I picked out a red-and-grey Hun, and followed him round as he took avoiding action, but kept above him while waiting my chance for a burst. It was a free-for-all as usual, with planes flashing like fireworks, and I was concentrating on getting a bead on my Hun while in a very tight vertical turn, and had just sent in one burst, which went in half-way up his fuselage, when – rak-ak-ak-ak! Tracers spitting past my head. Joystick right back, full right rudder, a twist of a spin, dive and zoom, and suddenly I realised that the sky was crowded with aeroplanes, all Albatroses, all thirsting for our blood.

I had a maniacal two minutes, skidding to left, to right, diving, zooming, and generally throwing the poor old Pup around like a drunk on skates. I must admit I began to quake, as we didn't seem to have a hope in hell, but I managed to find a spare second to touch wood, and I also put in a snatch burst whenever a Hun whizzed past my nose. We Pups all lost height quickly, with D–Vs buzzing over and among us like a swarm of wasps, to the tune of a continuous rattle of guns, with tracer criss-crossing all over the sky.

It was incredible that we escaped, and the main reason was that

Unsere
Flieger-Helden

Winners of the coveted *Ordre pour le Mérite* or Blue Max on a German postcard. The French were the first to introduce the 'ace' system but the Germans refined it with several gradations. The Blue Max was the highest award that a German flyer could gain.

there were so many of them they got in each other's way, but somehow it all ended and we weren't even badly shot about, thanks to the Pups' amazing manœuvrability. Two of the 'A' Flight types were driven down to 300 feet, and had to slither westwards to safety among the tree-tops. Scott and I were also lucky to get away, as he had a gun jam, and my engines started to miss and vibrate badly . . .

The Pup needed special skills to get the best out of its manœuvrability. Although McCudden had found that: 'The Sopwith could out-manœuvre any Albatros no matter how good the German pilot was . . . when it came to manœuvring,

The very popular
Sopwith Pup which
was first issued to the
RNAS in the autumn
of 1916. On account
of its lightness of
construction the
Pup was the most
manœuvrable of all
the First World War
fighters.

the Sopwith could turn twice to the Albatros' once.' There
were few pilots of McCudden's ability. The majority were
trained and had experienced only the slow and stable observation aircraft that made up the mass of RFC equipment.
Flick-turns, side-stepping, flying (and shooting) inverted,
were still an unknown world to the majority of RFC pilots.
And during the winter those few who had the experience and
courage to force their obsolete aircraft into these attitudes, were
gradually worn down by *Jastas*. Cruickshank, Sanday, Pale-
thorpe, Miller, were gallant officers whose names never entered
the role of aces that was a feature of the later years of the war.
They perished in out-classed and clumsy aircraft.

Arrogant in their immunity, the German aces decorated
their aircraft in ever more flamboyant colour schemes. It was
the last example of the tribal application of war paint – to
identify the chiefs and to strike terror in the hearts of the
enemy. The lower surfaces of the Albatri were kept sky blue
to conceal them while they climbed to dive from the sun, but
the fuselage and the tops of the wings were streaked gold,
purple, green and adorned with ancient or symbolic hiero-
glyphs. Karl Allmenröder of *Jasta 2* was the first to paint his
aircraft completely red; Hermann Goering of *Jasta 27* all black
with a white tail fin; Ernst Udet gold with yellow spinner;
Bruno Lörzer gold with a black tail and a white spinner.
Other pilots adorned their engine cowlings with hideous faces
or printed their names in enormous letters on the upper wing
surfaces so that their opponents should remember and quail.
Kempf of *Jasta 12* emphasized his by printing under his
name '*Kennscht mi noch?*' ('Do you not remember me?').

Now throughout the RFC a general decline in flying standards and tactics set in. The effects were felt all the way back to the training schools where pupils were often rushed through without a proper grounding in order that they should fill the depleted ranks of the squadrons in France. Many of the replacements sent to squadrons in the spring of 1917 arrived with less than twenty hours solo flying in their log books and often with only two or three hours on the type of aircraft which they were expected to fly in combat. Many too had contrived to get through their passing-out test without executing the more difficult of the basic manœuvres – like the right turn (when the response of the controls was severely affected by the flywheel effect of the rotating engine components and the airscrew). They were prone to such beginners' errors as letting the machine's nose fall during a turn or allowing the airspeed to sink to stalling point in a climb.

Squadron commanders testing the new recruits in mock combat as they arrived were horrified to find that they would even forget the transition of rudder to aileron effect in a steep bank. In these mock combats, staged deep behind the lines in the long spring evenings, the recruits would sometimes spin out of control and crash to their death without even having heard their guns fired in anger.

As the days of 1917 lengthened, the Germans with their stricter training schedules and the rigid flying discipline of their tightly knit formations increased their dominance of the air space over the whole length of the British sector. German tactics also were more sophisticated. The British were tied to

Werner Voss's Fokker triplane decorated with a face on the engine cowling. Voss was an expert with the triplane, a very manœuvrable but difficult plane to fly, and in it shot down twenty-two British planes in twenty-one days.

Flight sergeant in a BE 2C fitted with a camera for aerial photography. As late as 1917 the High Command considered that the chief function of the RFC was the collection of information rather than mastery of the skies.

the requirements of Corps and Army HQ. The Army Staff persisted in seeing the Flying Corps as an adjunct of their own intelligence and artillery branches, and where bombers or reconnaissance flights failed to achieve the objectives set them, their escorts were blamed. Thus the British fighter strength was tied to providing cumbersome escorts flying on slow and steady courses at medium altitude while the German Circuses were able to roam free in stepped-up tiers reaching to 15,000 feet.

But to use the word 'fighter' in any description of RFC equipment in 1916–17 was a misnomer. The fast single-seater 'scout', of which the Albatros was the prime example but which had its counterparts in the RNAS Pups and Triplanes, was a design-concept not wholly appreciated by the RFC Staff. The RFC 'brass' still regarded the proper role of the flying machine as that of an extension of cavalry reconnaissance which, like a cavalry squadron, should have the ability to raid or defend itself, but whose *raison d'être* was collecting information. For this purpose what was required – namely a stable, two-man aircraft which could be flown 'hands off' while the crew examined the ground, wrote notes, drew maps and leaned over the side to change plates in the mahogany box-camera – was the antithesis of what was needed to contest for mastery of the skies in close combat.

The Superintendent at Farnborough (Mervyn O'Gorman) was, like so many energetic Civil Servants, an ambitious Empire builder. Not only did he confine the work of the drawing offices strictly to this obsolete concept of design, but he was also at pains to ensure by the placing of contracts and

Building wings in an
aeroplane factory
during the First
World War.

other means, that no other aspirant manufacturer could produce a design – still less an aeroplane – whose merits might
rival or eclipse those of the Royal Aircraft Factory. Fortunately,
the chaotic state of this new industry, together with the vigour
and long sightedness of the Admiralty and its First Lord,
Winston Churchill, did allow, in these early years, firms such
as Short, Sopwith, Bristol and De Havilland, to survive and
produce rival designs. None the less, O'Gorman was tenacious
in his hostility, doing his best to restrict the output of rivals
through the Supply Directorate (which was answerable to him)
and, wherever possible, recommending against their adoption
for squadron service.

Now, in February of 1917, the 'new' aircraft product of the
Royal Aircraft Factory's design staff was about to enter
service. This was the RE 8, an ugly and perverse aircraft that
came to be so hated by its pilots that they would deliberately
try and 'crack them up' on landing or delivery, even though
this meant further long spells with worn out and obsolete
equipment.

The RE 8 embodied practically every major body design
fault which had already been identified and for which the cure
was known. The fin area was small and had to undergo suc-
cessive modifications in service to make it safe; and the undercarriage was set too far back relative to the aircraft's centre of
gravity and it was easy to 'put the nose in' when landing on
rough ground – with highly disagreeable consequences; and
the placing of the large air scoop just above the engine severely
curtailed the pilot's forward view and gave the machine
dangerous stalling characteristics.

Another design, a bomber, from the private De Havilland concern, the DH 4, was going into service at almost the same moment and yet another two-seater, the Bristol Fighter, was on the way. But the DH 4 had been designed round a Rolls-Royce engine and demand for this superb engine was so high that the De Havilland airframes had to be fitted with an engine designed by the Royal Aircraft Factory. This had a lower power output and had been rushed into production by O'Gorman in its original form (in spite of the engineer staff recommending some fifty-seven different modifications to such major items as pistons and valve gear).

Opposite above The RE 8 reconnaissance machine which was introduced late in 1916 and remained in service in large numbers until the Armistice despite its many shortcomings.

Below An RE 8 of No. 52 Squadron about to set out.

With the first deliveries of the RE 8 in France, its evil reputation, magnified by disappointment among crews who had pinned their hopes on its arrival, spread rapidly through the RFC: 52 Squadron, relative novices, were the first to receive the aeroplane and promptly lost four of their pilots from uncontrollable spins set off by the minimal fin area. Morale sank so low that an exchange was ordered between 52 and 34 (a more experienced squadron still flying the BE 2Es). Soon another unpleasant characteristic of the RE 8 emerged:

When a bad landing threw an aircraft on to its nose, there was almost a certainty of fire. The engine was pushed back into the emergency and petrol tanks so that the whole of the spirit flowed over the engine, and in the fires which resulted, many pilots and observers perished.

The C.O. of 34 Squadron issued some 'notes for the guidance of pilots' and their text has survived:

The chief thing to remember is that the machine gives very little indication of losing its speed until it suddenly shows an uncontrollable tendency to dive which cannot be corrected in time if you are near the ground.

You will find the rudder control in every case of spinning or swinging tail will become very stiff, and you may not be able to get it very central but you should aim (without putting on sufficient pressure to break anything) to do this.

With the engine off the thing to avoid is gliding too slowly. At 65 m.p.h. or below, when gliding, the machine suddenly loses speed. This is particularly the case when making a turn to enter the aerodrome as the extra resistance caused by the rudder is sufficient to bring down the pace. . . .

One more point as regards losing speed. Observers must be cautioned that when an aeroplane is gliding down from work over the lines they must not stand up in order to look over the pilot's shoulder for the fun of the thing, as the extra head resistance caused may lead to the aeroplane falling below its critical gliding speed, and so bring about an accident.

It was bad enough in routine flying, but in combat the RE 8

was a death trap. Not untypical was the experience of 59 Squadron, newly equipped in April of 1917, which sent out six of its RE 8s at 8.15 a.m. to photograph the Drocourt-Quéant switch line; caught by *Jasta 11* over Vietrie. All six were shot down and ten of the pilots and observers were killed.

That winter then, the British Air Staff were faced with a threefold problem. In addition to reviving the flagging morale of the squadron in the field, they had to evolve and produce a single-seat fighter with speed, manœuvrability and armament superior to the enemy; and they had to ensure that the impact that this machine would make on its first arrival should not be wasted by unskilled or incompetent pilots.

The previous year the first of a new and technically highly advanced engine had been delivered to the RFC. This was the Hispano-Suiza 8A. A V8 with aluminium monobloc castings and threaded steel liners that gave 140 h.p. at 1,400 r.p.m., yet weighed only 330 lbs. One was installed experimentally in a BE 2C, transforming the speed and rate of climb of that sleepy aircraft. But the aerodynamic characteristics of the BE 2 made it completely unsuitable for dog-fighting no matter how much power the engine developed and it was plain that the airframe would have to be radically modified. At first drawings (designated FE 10) were for a 'pusher' aircraft like the BE 9 but this was plainly obsolete before it reached even the prototype stage.

A second design, designated SE 5, was more promising. It was for a rakish, square-rigged, single-seater, neither as streamlined nor as aesthetically pleasing as the Albatros, but light and rugged-looking, offering an excellent pilot view. The 'new' design was still recognizably from the lineage of the BE 2 and the RE 8, lacking the instant agility of the Sopwith single-seaters. But O'Gorman's design staff were inspired by a different design philosophy claiming that stability which they had formerly offered as being essential for observation would now pay dividends in making the new design a steady 'gun platform'.

Under constant pressure from the RFC staff, the design, development and production stages merged dangerously close. On 20 November 1916 the prototype was submitted for final inspection and the approved note was issued at 21.30 hours that evening. Detail developments and intermittent flight trials continued at Farnborough for the next three weeks and on Christmas Eve the test pilot, Major F.W. Goodden, took the second prototype across to France where it was tried by selected pilots from the Nieuport and Spad squadrons of the RFC.

The SE 5A, which proved to be one of the most successful fighter planes of the war.

Goodden brought the aeroplane back to England on 4 January and made one more flight on the twenty-sixth. That Sunday he turned up at 11 a.m. for a 'joy ride' and took off from the still frosty runway at 11.10 a.m. Eight minutes later, having made two circuits, when he was approaching to land from the southeast, the aircraft broke up in the air and Goodden lost his life. An official inquiry blamed the airscrew and these findings were published. But investigation of the wreckage continued while the production examples were being built and it emerged that the airscrew was not to blame, but that the drawing had left out the web elements for the wing so that after a certain flying time, the struts pulled out of the wing surface.

In March, the first of the production series SE 5 arrived at Martlesham for service testing. The report was pessimistic:

Lateral control insufficient, especially poor at low speeds. The machine manœuvred poorly, and was almost uncontrollable below 70 m.p.h. in gusts, causing a crash on take-off on 29.3.17. The windscreen, unnecessarily large, hindered the pilot's landing view.

These comments, together with data for turning time and other manœuvrability factors, did not augur well for the SE 5's first encounter with the enemy. None the less, the plan and the aircraft itself had gone too far for any drawing back. In March of 1917, the whole of the RFC had been combed for its most skilful, most experienced and most aggressive pilots, to form the nucleus of a new RFC fighter arm built round the new fighter. Some, like Albert Ball, were taken off Nieuports. Others, like Cecil Lewis, off Moranes and others like Rhys-Davids, off the Spad. All were recalled to England and constituted as a new squadron, No. 56, stationed at London Colney. Here they were confined for six weeks to familiarize themselves with each other, their individual flying skills and tactics, and their new aeroplane.

To begin with it was unpopular. All agreed that the cumbersome 'greenhouse' – a multi-sided windscreen of celluloid and metal frame – obstructed the pilot's view and quickly became scratched and covered in oil. The Lewis gun mounted on the upper plane was virtually impossible to reload owing to gravitational pull and wind resistance. Ball was particularly outspoken:

The SE 5 has turned out a dud. Its speed is only about half Nieuport speed and it is not so fast in getting up. It is a great shame, for everybody thinks they are so good and expects such a lot from them. Well, I am making the best of a bad job. I am taking one gun off in order to take off weight. Also I am lowering the windscreen in order to take off resistance. A great many things I am taking off in the hopes that I shall get a little better control and speed. But it is a rotten machine . . .

Had the pilots of 56 Squadron remained in France, it is probable that all would have been killed in that spring. The average life of the fighter pilot had been reduced to less than a fortnight and, between March and May, 1,270 aeroplanes from RFC squadrons were destroyed.

As the terrible weeks of 'Bloody April' went by, the individual pilots at London Colney gradually came to terms with the new aircraft in the immunity of the Kentish sky. Each got his fitter to modify his own aeroplane as it suited him. Some removed the 'greenhouse' altogether. Ball, always obsessed with speed, removed not only the 'greenhouse', but also the top Lewis gun and lowered his seating position by eight inches.

Every day there was at least four hours flying practice. Formation, diving, basic combat manœuvres and follow-my-leader. The maximum speed of the SE 5 was 120 m.p.h. at 6,500 feet, falling below 100 m.p.h. at 15,000 feet. (Ball was wrong – the SE 5 was faster than his Nieuport 17 by nearly 15 m.p.h.) The pilots found that the aircraft could climb to 6,500 feet in eight minutes and to 10,000 feet in under fifteen minutes (both these figures were superior to the Albatros although, naturally, this was not known at the time). Furthermore, the SE 5 had an endurance of two and a half hours – nearly one hour more than the Albatros, so that 56 Squadron would have time to wait at maximum altitude for their enemy to appear below them. They found, too, that the stability of the aeroplane had several advantages, particularly in these last critical seconds when the enemy was in your gunsight. Confidence spread and with it an impatience to return to France. While they waited, the pilots would amuse themselves with evermore hair-raising aerobatics – a favourite trick was to roll the wheels on the sloping roof of number 3 hangar on the run-in in order to get a smoother landing.

On 7 April, at 11 a.m., the Squadron were ranged in line on the turf of London Colney warming up their engines. The night

before, a farewell party had been staged in the Black Swan at Radlett and, on the way back, Captain Foot, the leader, had crashed in a Metallurgique car and broken three ribs so the flight to their aerodrome at Vergaland was to be led by Cecil Lewis, the MC and former Morane pilot, who had celebrated his nineteenth birthday a month before.

There was a small group of parents and friends, and a few of the girls who had been at the Black Swan to wave them goodbye. Lewis taxied across to the eastern corner of the airfield with the other ten following behind him in single file. Turning into the wind, they took-off, banked and roared back over the sheds for a last wave at the little group on the tarmac. Then, climbing into V-formation, 56 Squadron headed for the channel coast. The day of the great encounter with Richthofen's Circus was but four weeks away.

A group of No. 56 Squadron officers in April 1917. Back row, left to right: G. J. C. Maxwell, N. B. Melville, H. M. T. Lehmann, C. R. N. Knight, L. M. Barlon and K. T. Kraggs. Front row, left to right: C. A. Lewis, J. O. Leach, R. G. Blomfield, A. Ball and R. T. C. Hoidge.

Bombing squadron on
its way to Germany
flying in Vee
formation.

CHAPTER SEVEN

Squadrons

I hope he roasted the whole way down.
Mick Mannock on hearing of Richthofen's death

While the Royal Flying Corps suffered under the flail of the Albatros Circuses in the early part of 1917, there was one sector where the Germans hesitated to venture. In the far north of Flanders the naval squadrons equipped with the Sopwith Triplane dominated the skies. The various administrative and design disputes that lay behind the immense superiority in equipment which the Navy held over the RFC have been mentioned. But in the spring of 1917, the paradox had resulted that the airspace over the quietest sector of the front was dominated by the English while that over the most active was the province of the German Circuses.

Finally, the slaughter of the regular RFC had become so serious that after much departmental obstruction a single squadron of Triplanes, 'Naval Ten', was moved on 4 June and put under No. 11 Wing RFC, being stationed at Droglandt. On their first day they were in action, shooting down two Albatri. Further encounters followed on 5th, 6th, 14th, 15th, 17th and 18th and in every one of them the Triplanes had the measure of their opponents.

'Naval Ten's' career was short and spectacular. Its core was the five Canadian Pilots, Raymond Collishaw, W.M. Alexander, G.E. Nash, E.V. Reid and J.E. Sharman who formed the 'Black Flight', painting their engine cowlings, metal fuselage panels and wheel covers in black gloss and carrying the name emblazoned in white, *Black Maria*, *Black Prince*, *Black Roger*, *Black Sheep* and *Black Death*.

Word had spread rapidly among the German pilots of these extraordinary little aeroplanes with their freakish head-on silhouette and their unnatural ability to climb and weave. A disturbing rumour arose that the Triplane could not be engaged by the normal tail approach – to do so was certain death for it could out-manœuvre any other plane in level flight, sliding round to sit on its adversary's rudder as if attached by a tow-line. But surely there was one unit that could cow these insolent new-comers? The all-red aeroplanes of Richthofen's

Sopwith Triplanes of No. 8 Squadron of the RNAS. With these planes the Naval Squadrons dominated their own sector in the early part of 1917.

Jasta 11 were given priority orders to seek out the 'Black Flight'.

For five days the Circus ranged up and down across the Ypres salient searching for their enemy. All the German anti-aircraft crews had been alerted to scan for the Triplanes and contact *Jasta 11* by telephone, but identification from the ground was difficult as in plane view the silhouette was much like that of the Sopwith Pup. Finally on 25 June, the two teams met over Quesnoy. On this patrol *Jasta 11* was commanded by Karl Allmenröder, Richthofen's twenty-two-year-old deputy who had been awarded the 'Blue Max' only ten days before. His Albatros was identified by his white engine cowl and spinner and white painted elevators. The encounter that followed was brief. The *Jasta* found that everything they had heard about the Triplane was true. Only Allmenröder himself scored a victory, shooting down *Black Sheep* (Nash) and then leading the *Jasta* away in a long dive which could outstrip the slower Triplanes.

The Canadian ace, Raymond Collishaw. He was the leader of the famous Triplane 'Black Flight', composed entirely of Canadians and one of the most successful fighter units of the war.

For two days the German pilots anxiously discussed tactics. Allmenröder decided to split the *Jasta* in two, flying one half at maximum altitude, the other lower than was normal in order to draw the Triplanes down. If the timing was right, the upper formation should be able to choose their own targets in the ensuing dive and rescue their comrades before the Triplanes 'locked on'. The matter was put to the test on 27 June, two days later. But something went wrong for the upper formation did not spot the attacking Triplanes until too late. 'Black Flight', again led by Collishaw, made one pass at the lower *Jasta* and then disappeared to the east. Observers on the ground saw the Albatri regain formation and start climbing with the exception of one aircraft with a white spinner and cowl which was gliding slowly westwards. Gradually the glide steepened and the Albatros fell into a vertical and uncontrollable dive. *Jasta 11* had lost its deputy. On the same day the 'Black Flight' claimed three more victims, two of them going down under the guns of Collishaw's *Black Maria*; and for the first three weeks in July it continued to wreak havoc among the now thoroughly disconcerted Circuses.

On 6 July 1917 Richthofen attacked a combined squadron of FE 2s and RE 8s escorted by the 'Black Flight'. Collishaw got one of the Albatri. Richthofen himself broke through the escort and attacked a 'Fee' head-on, crewed by Captain D.C. Cunnell (killed a few days later) with gunner Lieutenant A.E. Woodbridge. Woodbridge kept his nerve and filled the Albatros engine with lead. Richthofen, temporarily blinded, just managed to put the aeroplane down right side up and then fainted with a head wound, remaining in hospital for a month.

But no five men, however brave, could stand up indefinitely to the full weight of the angry *Jastas*. *Black Death* was set on fire on 22 July and Sharman was killed. *Black Roger* went down with Reid on 28th. On 30th, *Black Maria* was also shot down although Collishaw had already been recalled to England to serve for a period as instructor (he ended the war with sixty-three victims), and the gallant little company was disbanded. By this time the first of the Sopwith Camels (in essence a more powerful and robust Pup) were being delivered to the naval squadrons and the Triplane, with its critical servicing problems was being phased out. The brief and brilliant career of the 'Tripehound' did leave one ironic legacy however. When the Germans had developed their own Triplane, the Fokker Dr I (both Richthofen and Hoeppner had gone on record with the belief that the Sopwith Triplane was the best English fighter of the war), many RFC crews recognized (as they believed) its friendly silhouette, withheld their fire and allowed the enemy to close the range until too late to save their lives. . . .

It soon became apparent that the Sopwith Camel,* although very difficult for a novice to fly, could be mastered by any of the more experienced pilots, and was so agile and quick in combat that it had to be ordered in quantity for the RFC as an alternative to the SE 5. However, during the summer of 1917, Camel deliveries were slow and the only hope of dealing with the Albatros Circuses was the SE 5.

On 7 April 56 Squadron had arrived at their base at Vertgaland and spent two weeks on navigation flights, gunnery testing and tuning their machines. Professionalism was now at its peak and combat tactics a formidable synthesis of individual flair and group discipline. On this subject James McCudden, coolest of all the British aces, wrote:

I consider it a patrol leader's work to pay more attention to the main points affecting the fight than to do all the fighting himself. The main points are: (1) arrival of more EA who have tactical advantage, i.e. height; (2) patrol drifting too far east; (3) patrol getting below bulk of enemy formation. As soon as any of these circumstances occur, it is time to take advantage of the SE's superior speed over EA scouts and break off the fight, rally behind leader and climb west of EA until you are above them before attacking them again.

On 22 April the Squadron flew their first offensive sortie on a trail that was to bring them to their quarry, and disaster, within less than three weeks.

The first encounter was highly successful. Albert Ball shot down two Albatri and other members of the Squadron got two more. For the rest of April and the first week in May, 56

* The Camel eventually became the most successful fighter of the war, Camel pilots shooting down 1,294 enemy machines. It was the first British fighter to have twin Vickers guns, and it was the hump made by the cowling over their breeches that led to the nickname of Camel, which became so prevalent that it was adopted as the machine's official name. All the major weight components were gathered into the forward seven feet of the fuselage, which gave the Camel a remarkable agility, as the moments of inertia were so small. But this, combined with the torque of its rotary engine, gave the Camel its most famous quality – the ability to turn to the right in only half the time it took other fighters. Delivery began in July 1917 and ended after 5,490 had been built.

Above The Sopwith Camel, first brought into service in the middle of 1917. Although it had some idiosyncrasies, once they had been mastered it was found to be the ideal fighting plane. It was the first British plane to have twin Vickers guns.

Left James McCudden, who joined the RFC in 1913 and made his first operational flight as a pilot in July 1915. He scored fifty-seven victories before his death in July 1918 at the age of twenty-two. He won more decorations than any other member of the RFC, RNAS or RAF during the war.

Albert Ball, seated in his SE 5. On 7 April 1917 he went to France with No. 56 Squadron, the first unit to be equipped with the SE 5, and it was in this plane, exactly one month later, that he met his death.

Squadron cut a fine swath in the German Air Service. As the pilots' confidence grew, they became accustomed to attacking against odds of up to three-to-one. Ball was indefatigable, he still kept his old Nieuport and would sortie alone in this when the SE 5 was being serviced, being over four hours a day in the air. At fighting altitudes the SE 5 was still outclimbed by the Albatros, but the very high quality of the pilots and the consternation which they created among their enemy, who had been enjoying such total superiority up to that time, gave them an advantage. They must have clashed several times with *Jasta 11* for mention of 'all red scouts' can be traced many times in the Squadron log, but they never found Richthofen himself at full strength until their second patrol on 7 May.

It was a still evening, but the sky was heavy with threatening masses of cumulus cloud towering from four to twelve thousand feet; 56 Squadron flew at full strength – eleven machines in formation, two fours and a three, and found their enemy at 18,000 feet behind the German lines.

How far this was a deliberately contrived ambush, how far an accident arising from the Squadron's over-confidence, will never be known. The fact remains that McCudden took the whole Squadron into a dive after six Albatri of a different *Jasta* that were flying east, 3,000 feet below. But Richthofen himself and two *Jastas* of *JG I* were flying at the same altitude some one-to-three miles distant and followed 56 Squadron down. The battle broke up into individual contests and within minutes each of the highly skilled pilots of 56 Squadron was fighting for his life, turning ever tighter and more desperately, losing altitude, separated from his fellows. For over an hour the Squadron struggled to save itself, fighting down from 15,000 feet to 600 before, in fading light, the survivors ducked and weaved their way individually back to Vertgaland. Of the eleven SE 5s that had gone out on that evening patrol on 7 May, only five returned. Ball himself, the indestructible,* was missing with his score standing at forty-three – by far the highest at that time, of any pilot in the RFC.

There is a strange irony in that 56 Squadron, forged as the head of the lance which was to break the power of the Albatros *Jasta* and, in particular, to kill Richthofen, should have been the instrument that eliminated Richthofen's closest rival.

At 18.00 hours on the evening of 23 September 1917, the day of the autumnal equinox, cloud-base was at an altitude of 9,000 feet. Werner Voss's *Jasta* had flown its last patrol of the day under his leadership and he was up in his own Triplane, eyes focused on the red glow of the sunset that would silhouette any stragglers who might be making for the safety of the British lines.

A few minutes after reaching operational altitude, Voss spotted his prey and dived after it, but above him and invisible against the darkening sky of the east was a flight from 56 Squadron of six of its most experienced pilots – R.T.C. Hoidge, A.P.F. Rhys-Davids, R.A. Mayberry, V.P. Cronyn, and K.K. Muspratt, led by James McCudden, V.C. Although fast in a climb the Triplane was no match for the SE 5A in a dive, and the six Englishmen rapidly gained on Voss before he could get within shooting distance of his selected victim. Rhys-Davids and McCudden split to put themselves either side of Voss's Triplane so that one or the other would catch him if he tried to bank out of trouble. Muspratt and Hoidge parted vertically so that either a climb or dive by Voss would offer a target, while the other two SE 5As hung back as guards. Yet before the leaders could open fire, some sixth sense had warned

---

* The exact manner of his death is still a mystery, as with so many other aces of the war. He was last seen diving after an Albatros. Some days later the Germans claimed that he had been shot down by the brother of Manfred von Richthofen, Lothar, who had a meteoric career at the front shooting down four Allied aircraft. But on that day, Lothar claimed a Triplane, and was supported by several of his comrades.

Werner Voss was commander of *Jasta 10* of Richthofen's Circus. He was killed in September 1917 in an encounter with a flight from No. 56 Squadron. McCudden said of Voss in his last battle: 'His flying is wonderful, his courage magnificent and in my opinion he is the bravest German airman whom it has been my privilege to see.'

Voss, and he straightened out of his dive, performing at the same time an incredibly rapid flick-turn that brought him face-to-face with his four converging enemies. For split seconds the adversaries confronted each other at a closing speed of 180 m.p.h. Startled, the English all opened fire, but none of the bullets struck their target and even as the SE 5As passed above and below him and to his right and left, Voss was giving the Triplane right rudder which brought him round on Hoidge's tail. For a few seconds the English strained eyes against the failing light, then the orange stab of flame from the Triplane's twin Spandaus showed Voss's position as he filled Hoidge's fuselage with bullets.

The SE 5As, perfectly disciplined, and with the advantage of speed built up in their dive, climbed and banked again to position themselves in the lethal 'box' from which this time there would be no escape. Yet again the Triplane turned before the British could open fire and, raising his nose, Voss slipped through the descending formation, this time riddling McCudden's aircraft and turning immediately, put himself on the tail of Muspratt, the last man in the flight. Three times the sequence repeated itself until the British discarded their advantage in numbers and formation and challenged Voss individually and in pairs.

By now most of the SE 5As had emptied their Lewis guns and few of the pilots had found the time to re-load, continuing to rely on the single belt-fed Vickers that fired through the airscrew. The light was failing and an easterly breeze which had risen in the evening carried the fight back over the lines. There was still time for one more pass at this indomitable foe.

A. P. F. Rhys-Davids, one of the several experienced pilots who were drafted to No. 56 Squadron. It was his guns which brought down Voss's Triplane in September 1917.

Rhys-Davids, tense with the effort of anticipating the Triplane's next evasion, found in one magic instant that it remained in his sights. Hardly believing his luck, Rhys-Davids closed the range while Voss's figure in the cockpit enlarged to fill the ring-sight. Still the Triplane flew straight and level. Somewhere, at some point, Voss had been badly wounded and had either fainted or was incapable of working the controls. Rhys-Davids fired a long burst on deflection raking the whole length of the Triplane's fuselage. For a second the German aircraft wobbled and then the nose fell, engine full on, screaming vertical and then over-vertical, until against the velvet of the darkened landscape below a dark red flash exploded, brighter than any shell-burst as Voss's Triplane smashed into a thousand fragments.

Sioux head, the
insignia of the
Escadrille Americaine,
the American
volunteer unit which
joined the French Air
Force in April 1916.

CHAPTER EIGHT
Braves

Elijah was reputed to be the patron saint of aviators, but as he went to Heaven in a chariot of fire, this was something we weren't too keen about.

Kiffin Rockwell

Of all the units that took part in the dog fights over the Western Front none had such individual character as the *Escadrille Americaine* of the French Air Force. It was the creation and the club of a number of widely different, yet in their varying ways typical, Americans, having in common only bravery, a taste for adventure and a United States passport. Playboys, soldiers-of-fortune and professional aviators came and went in its ranks. They flew Nieuports and then Spad single-seaters that displayed an Indian brave's head as unit insignia.

The squadron had originated in the minds of a number of adventurous Americans, but the driving idea was that of a New Englander, Norman Prince, one of the few American citizens to earn a pilot's licence before the outbreak of war. Prince had travelled to France in the winter of 1914 with the intention of forming a unit for American volunteer flyers. In Paris he had teamed up with Edmund Gros, a rich doctor who had built up the American Ambulance Field Service. The two men set about combing all the various units to which American volunteers had been drawn in those romantic opening months of the war (and where in most cases they were by now thoroughly disillusioned and miserable).

At first the French authorities were obstructive. But with the deadlock on the ground and the increasing propaganda value of the personal side of aerial warfare, their opposition changed to support. Seven Americans were enlisted and given the acting rank of NCO in a squadron commanded by two French officers. The *Escadrille* was officially formed on 16 April 1916. In addition to Prince there was William Thaw, who had owned a hydroplane while still at Yale; Kiffin Rockwell, a medical student from North Carolina; and Victor Chapman, a Harvard graduate who had been at the École des Beaux Arts in Paris and had joined the Foreign Legion as a private when war broke out. (Both these two had grandfathers who had been

The original members of the *Escadrille Americaine* at Luxeuil: (from left to right) Kiffin Rockwell, Georges Thénault, Norman Prince, Alfred de Laage de Meux, Elliot Cowdin, Bert Hall (in black engineer's uniform), James McConnell and Victor Chapman. Not visible, behind Thénault, is William Thaw.

officers in the Confederate Army.) In addition there were two from the Ambulance Service, James McConnell and Elliot Cowdin, and a tough Texan, Bert Hall, who had made his name as a pre-war stunt flyer and had already acquitted himself valiantly in the French Air Force, having captured a Halberstadt two-seater by forcing it to land behind the French lines. Of these original seven, only three survived. Altogether thirty-eight American flyers passed through the ranks of the *Escadrille* of whom nine were killed and two invalided out with wounds.

The first posting for the squadron was at Luxeuil in the Vosges. The French authorities could not decide on the balance between tactical deployment and propaganda. The American flyers were given every luxury. In spite of their status as 'other ranks' and minuscule pay scale, money flowed freely, both in grants and from their private incomes. They were quartered in a sumptuous villa next to the Roman Baths and messed with their officers at the best hotel in the town. For many weeks the *Escadrille* was carefully nursed and committed to action only when the dice were heavily loaded in its favour. All the time the French propaganda machine dwelt on their achievements.

The pilots' spirits found vent in extravagant and destructive sackings of the local inns and in repeated 'blow-outs' in Paris.

One of the earliest members of the unit, James McConnell (who was later to die in battle) wrote with foreboding: 'I thought of the luxury we were enjoying; our comfortable beds, baths, and motorcars, and I recalled the ancient custom of giving the man selected for the sacrifice a royal time of it before the appointed day.'

And indeed that day was not far away. The fall of Fort Vaux at Verdun in June 1916 caused tremors that threatened to bring down the whole of the Verdun system. In this dreadful battle of attrition the long-range artillery piece was king, and whosoever could give it eyes and lengthen its range would win the day. The *Escadrille* was a Nieuport squadron and only the Nieuport could cope with the Fokker which, in turn, was protecting the German artillery spotting balloons. Its commitment became inevitable.

It was here, over the blackened earth of the Verdun trench system with its permanent haze of sulphur and cordite fumes that the élite of the German air strength, led by Oswald Boelcke and Max Immelmann, was engaged. On the evening of 24 May, the machine of one of the pioneers of the *Escadrille*, William Thaw, who had started the war with the Foreign Legion, was shot to pieces in a duel with three Fokkers and he crash-landed with his pectoral artery cut open, to survive in hospital. On 25th, another original member, Bert Hall was badly wounded. On 17 June Victor Chapman narrowly survived a duel with Boelcke, being wounded in the head. On 18 June Thaw's replacement, Clyde Balsley, was struck in the thigh by an incendiary bullet and taken to a field hospital where he contracted gangrene. The same week, Chapman – still flying, though with his head in bandages – was caught in failing light by five Fokkers and shot down, the first American airman to be killed in the war. Now only Kiffin Rockwell, Elliot Cowdin and the founder, Norman Prince, remained. Within a month the carefree mood had gone sour. The pilots were forcing themselves beyond their capabilities and new arrivals were swept up mercilessly into a back-breaking routine of four or five patrols a day, stopping only in the ten o'clock twilight and starting again at dawn. After Chapman's death, Rockwell wrote to his brother: 'Prince and I are going to fly ten hours tomorrow and we'll do our best to kill one or two Germans for Victor.'

The following day, Rockwell, blinded by fatigue, was shot down by a German who dived on him from the noon sun. Less than a week later Prince stayed out too long and crashed into a high tension cable in the evening light as he followed the ground contours back to base.

Edward Rickenbacker, America's ace of aces. He joined the 94th Aero Squadron on 4 March 1918 and by the end of the war had scored twenty-six victories. With Raoul Lufbery and Douglas Campbell he made the first patrol over enemy lines by an American air unit.

Thus ended the first phase in the history of the *Lafayette Escadrille** (as it had come to be known), and those who decry the importance of the American contribution to the air war and point to the low scores of their 'aces' and the manner in which their first regular squadrons were so carefully husbanded and kept out of combat, should not forget the reckless heroism and devotion of those first pilots in the *Lafayette*. Two years were to pass before any other American airmen came even close to matching the deeds of this first gallant unit – and even then the US's latter-day aces, Frank Luke, Edward Rickenbacker, Joseph Wehner and the like, had to be trained in tactical matters by the French, who had learned from the *Lafayette*'s examples, and were equipped from the same source.

Before the advent of the Albatros and the Circuses and the prophetic duel between Richthofen and Lanoe Hawker, before the onset of 'Bloody April' and the decimation of the RFC squadrons, this small band of gallant volunteers had allowed themselves to be dashed to pieces against an enemy far better trained, and many times their number.

The attitude of the French Command then underwent a complete reversal. From husbanding the Americans in case the death of one of them should cause a reaction, they seem to

* The initial title of *Escadrille Americaine* was dropped following German pressure exercised through isolationist circles in the – at this time allegedly neutral – United States. The French then designated it by the simple code number N (Nieuport) 124. Claude Genet then had the idea of fixing on the name of '*Lafayette*' and this title stayed with the unit until 18 February 1918, when it was officially incorporated into the United States air arm.

Frank Luke Jr, the second highest scorer of the American aces, with the Spad in which he blazed a name for himself. He was known as the 'Balloon Buster' because of his remarkable success in destroying balloons; he busted fifteen before his death in September 1918.

have decided that a proflgate expenditure of American lives was a surer guarantee of a deeper commitment. Before the war when Sir Henry Wilson (later Chief of the Imperial General Staff) had asked General Joffre how many English soldiers he desired in the expeditionary force, the reply came back: 'Only one, but I will make sure that he is killed.' This philosophy seems for a time to have pervaded the French attitude to American flyers.

The *Escadrille* was expanded. Some hardened flyers like Raoul Lufbery and James Hall and Charles Nordhoff, joined their compatriots along with many others who had to learn from scratch.

French training schools were no bed of roses. We were up every morning before dawn, with only a cup of lukewarm chicory, masquerading as coffee, to sustain us till the first meal at eleven o'clock. Daylight found us shivering at our various fields, awaiting our turns on that fearful and wonderful contraption known as the Blériot monoplane.

Its construction was a source of never-ceasing wonder. With only a slight exaggeration, it seemed as if they were merely gathered-up odds and ends of wood, discarded matchsticks and the like, which were wired together, catch-as-catch-can fashion, with bailing wire to form the fuselage. Then old handkerchiefs were sewed together, to cover the wings and that part of the fuselage around the pilot's seat. The remainder of the fuselage was left naked, which gave the ship a sort of half-finished appearance. We were undoubtedly wrong in thinking it was left naked because, with true French thrift, they wanted to save on fabric. More likely it was to facilitate replacement of brace wires, which had an uncomfortable

Raoul Lufbery, the most brilliant star of the *Escadrille Lafayette*. Born in France of French parents, he emigrated to America with his family at the age of six. He is here shown wearing the decorations bestowed upon him by his country of birth.

habit of snapping when any particular strain was put on them.

The landing gear was fairly solid, with junior bicycle wheels at the end of each axle, wrapped with a couple of turns of light rubber cord.

Of the 209 American nationals who volunteered for service in the French Air Force the majority went through the training school at Buc, learning on the clipped-wing Blériots (the *Pingouins*) and graduating to twin-engined Caudron R IVs whose whole wing warped in a tight turn. But of these 209, only thirty-one actually found their way into the exclusive *Lafayette* squadron and the remainder served, until America joined the war, with other French front line units.

After its brutal mauling at Verdun, the *Escadrille* was taken out of the line for resting and re-equipped with the new Spad VII single-seater with a V8 Hispano-Suiza engine. At first there was a wide gulf between those who had been through the deadly Fokker battles of the summer and the brash young *arrivistes*. In the words of the official historian 'there was considerable disharmony at various times'. More, perhaps, than any other front line unit, the *Lafayette* seems to have been racked by fads and superstitions. There was a great craze for collecting golden medals and bracelets – but with the proviso that they had to be presented by one of the girls in Paris; then there was a wave of addiction to black, velvet cats – which had to emanate from the same source – without whose company in the cockpit it was dangerous even to take off. Every pilot carried a girl's silk stocking under his flying helmet: '. . . if anything happened to you it was a sure sign the girl didn't love you.'*

For nearly a year after the United States' entry into the war the *Lafayette Escadrille* continued to fly under French colours. In the latter months of 1917 the policy of conservation seems to have returned, although the publicity did not diminish.

In February of 1918 the *Escadrille* was formally absorbed into the United States Air Service and was redesignated the 103rd Aero Squadron. Although Thaw, who had survived his earlier wounding, remained commander, most of the first alumni were dispersed to stiffen other units. The squadron's mascot, a lion cub called Whisky, was sent to the zoo, the French uniforms were thrown away and orders were given that the slackness and indiscipline 'for which the unit was notorious' should be rectified.

Three months later the last link with the old days of the *Escadrille* were severed when Raoul Lufbery's Nieuport

---

* It is possible that this practice came from some of the French *Escadrilles* where it had originated with the French ace, Jean Navarre, who flew in winter time with a girl's stocking actually pulled over his head as a protection against the cold.

caught fire during combat in full view of his new command, the 94th US Squadron, at Maron, who were watching from the ground. Lufbery, who had always sworn that he would never burn, shut off the motor and coolly tried to extinguish the flames by sideslipping first to the left and then to the right. In a Spad it might have been possible, but with the short-nacelled rotaries like the Nieuport and the Camel, flames from the engine compartment would make the cockpit intolerable within a few seconds. Horrified, the onlookers saw Lufbery climb out and continue to try and operate the joystick while sitting on the head-fairing; then he crawled back along the fuselage towards the tail and let go, falling three thousand feet to his death.

All those characteristics of the First World War aircrew who flew and fought without parachutes, who knew that death from wounds would occur four times out of five, who saw their comrades come and go and measured their own existence by the hour, all these were personified in the members of the *Lafayette Escadrille*.

In addition, they were expatriates; they fought without a country, surrounded by people who spoke a different language and whose attachments and values were alien. Like the Polish squadrons in the Battle of Britain twenty-three years later, this seems to have heightened their ardour, but brought with it too a certain melancholy that is exemplified in their favourite mess song:

> We meet 'neath the sounding rafters,
>   The walls all around us are bare;
> They echo the peals of laughter;
>   It seems that the dead are there.
>
> So stand by your glasses steady,
>   This world is a world of lies.
> Here's a toast to the dead already;
>   Hurrah for the next man who dies.
>
> Cut off from the land that bore us,
>   Betrayed by the land that we find,
> The good men have gone before us,
>   And only the dull left behind.
>
> So stand by your glasses steady,
>   The world is a web of lies.
> Then here's to the dead already,
>   And hurrah for the next man who dies.

CHAPTER NINE

Storks

. . . will remain the purest symbol of the qualities of his race.
Indomitable tenacity, ferocious energy, sublime courage: animated
by the most resolute faith in victory, he bequeaths to the French
soldier an imperishable memory which will exalt the spirit of
sacrifice.

Guynemer memorial

The inscription is taken from the marble plaque on the
Guynemer memorial at the Panthéon in Paris. The sentiments
expressed, while wholly suitable to Georges Guynemer's
own tortured and mystic heroism, were less appropriate to the
majority of his colleagues among whom a kind of cynical
despair gradually took root – flowering with tragic consequence
in 1940.

The French had been the first to realize the immense
propaganda value of the air war and the manner in which, by
presenting it in personal terms as a series of individual contests,
public attention could be distracted from the futile carnage of
the trenches. 'The Knights of the air', wrote one commen-
tator, 'sally forth to do battle before the eyes of the assembled
hosts as did the chevalier of olden time.'

The French were the first to institute the 'ace' system (which
was of course never officially recognized in Britain, though in
Germany it was still further refined with several gradations
and the coveted *Pour le Mérite* or 'Blue Max' at the summit).
The rules of scoring were strict but if a pilot had five confirmed
victories (in May of 1917 this limit was raised to ten) he quali-
fied for the title of 'As' and was mentioned by name in
official communiqués.

An immediate and unfortunate growth of class differentia-
tion set in. It was virtually impossible for a pilot or gunner of a
two-seater to reach this score and among the single-seaters it
was far easier for the Nieuport pilots than any other. The
authorities encouraged the division by grouping the best
Nieuport pilots in one *Escadrille*. The original *Escadrille*
selected was N.3 and every pilot in it identified himself as being
one of that select company by painting a white stork in flight
on the side of his fuselage. As the aces multiplied propaganda

Opposite Georges
Guynemer, standing
in front of his Spad.
The stork on the side
of the plane was the
symbol of the
Cigognes Escadrille.

had a snowball effect. More of the *Cigognes Escadrilles* were formed and became a magnet to attract outstanding flyers from other units. (It is worth noting that the *Cigognes* were among the first to be re-equipped with the Spad, from early autumn 1916.)

Almost incidentally the French had chanced on the most effective system of tactical deployment of their single-seat fighter strength – putting into practice a conclusion which was reached somewhat later and on purely tactical grounds by Oswald Boelcke and General von Hoeppner. There is no doubt that the strength and gallantry of the *Cigognes* group was of critical importance during the Battle of Verdun. During May Boelcke, whose Fokkers were still operating in threes, was urging that larger *Jagdstaffeln* (the first use of the 'hunting pack' term) should be started. Had this been done there is little doubt that the *Cigognes* would have suffered the fate which was later to befall them over the Somme. But Max Immelmann's death on 18 June led to a personal order from the Kaiser that Boelcke should be grounded lest he too were to be lost to Germany, and the German ace had been sent on an inspection tour of the Russian front.

Probably the only unit in the French Air Service that could rival the *Cigognes* in reputation and extravagance was N.77, known as *Les Sportifs* on account of the number of sportsmen and playboys who passed through its ranks. One of its most famous was Maurice Boyau, captain of the French International Rugby team in 1914, and another Georges Boillot, the racing driver, who had fought so valiantly and lost to the three white Mercedes of the German team in the last Grand Prix before war was declared.

The *Escadrille N.77* was an exclusive club where the private incomes of the members lavishly supplemented their pay from the Republic. They brought their own servants and motor-cars and quartered their ladies in the most expensive hotels in the area. Their contacts and influences, particularly that of Capitaine l'Hermite, their Commanding Officer, ensured that both their equipment and publicity were the best. However, a critical examination of the score recorded by its members seems to indicate that although there were exceptions, the '*Sportifs*' seem to have spent most of their time shooting down balloons.*

In contrast the *Cigognes* were more desperate men and among them rivalries and loyalties burned fiercely. Some of them were poor, and had to subsist on their income as officers, but the system of grants from private sources which the Michelin brothers had started was an extra incentive to raise their tallies. The pace of living was furious: the *Cigognes* were

Opposite Michel Coiffard, France's most successful 'balloon-buster'. He destroyed twenty-eight balloons between January 1917, when he joined the Flying Corps, and his death in October 1918.

always surrounded by touts, pimps and salesmen of all kinds who set up quarters in the vicinity of their aerodromes. They were lionized in Parisian Society and hostesses would send their Delaunay limousines to wait beside the hangars so that when the pilots landed from the afternoon patrols their favourites could be hurried back to Paris in time for the night's festivities. Paris was the very hub of the alliance, her society uniquely self-important, over-flowing with money and with unlimited pleasures available.

Above Spad VII, powered by a Hispano-Suiza engine, the most famous of the French in-line-engined fighters. It was one of the war's outstanding aircraft and was flown by the air forces of nearly every Allied power.

Mistinguett was drawing huge crowds at the Folies-Bergères: the great Bernhardt, though aged and ailing, was still seductive as ever, dividing her time between the theatre and her hospital for the wounded at the Odéon: at the Opéra Comique *Manon* was all the rage, and in May, when the Germans were hammering their way on to Côte 304, there was a glittering film première of *Salammbô* and the Spring Flower Show was reinstated in all its pre-war glory.

In such a setting the glamorous airmen were prestigious toys to be courted and shown on every occasion.

During the autumn and winter of 1916–17 the *Cigognes Escadrilles* were being re-equipped with the Spad single-seater and their numbers (3, 26, 73, 103 and 167), now carried the

*Dating from the earliest period when observation was regarded as the primary role of the Air Arm, the destruction of a balloon was classified as a 'victory' and allowed to stand in a pilot's score sheet, and this was never altered. For though a balloon could not evade gunfire in a way an aircraft could, it was by way of compensation very well defended from the ground – a measure of its importance. 'Balloon-busting' was an extremely hazardous business, and attracted its own extraordinary aces, such as Heinrich Gontermann of Germany (18 balloons), Willy Coppens of Belgium (28), Frank Luke of the United States (15) and Michel Coiffard of France (28).

prefix 'SP' instead of 'N'. The change from the Nieuport symbolized their altered status. The little rotary engined sesquiplane, nimble, delicate, dependent on the pilot's skill for its effectiveness was infinitely rewarding to those who could excite its response, but would not tolerate clumsiness or cowardice. The Spad with its inline liquid-cooled engine was faster, but less agile; its orthodox construction made it stronger, but heavier. The storks on the side of the fuselage were now painted black,* and like the change from red to black on the Rolls-Royce, a legend arose that could be neither proven nor denied that it was an expression of mourning for their patron, Guynemer.

Georges Guynemer personified the dedicated and obsessive hero (*see* Chapter 5). But more typical is the rough and glamorous figure of Charles Nungesser. Seconded from the Hussars in 1914, he had already packed a life-time into his youth. He was a champion swimmer and boxer and had taken up motor cycling and automobile racing with ardour. He successfully flew an aeroplane solo on the very first occasion that he tried the controls and then decided to design his own. The outbreak of war put a stop to this, but in the first few weeks Nungesser distinguished himself, as a hussar, by way-laying a German Staff car behind the enemy lines, shooting the occupants and driving it across No-man's Land under fire from his own side. He was allowed to keep the car and was awarded the *Médaille Militaire*, but scorning both these he declared that his greatest wish was to be transferred to the Air Service.

For the next three years this extraordinary man went closer and more frequently into the arms of death than any other flyer of the First World War. After six adventurous months with a reconnaissance squadron in the north of France, his fire and courage brought him a transfer to a Nieuport *Escadrille* at Nancy. Flouting the superstitions that were rife among single-seater pilots, Nungesser adorned his Nieuport with the symbols of ill-omen. A coffin, two lighted candles, the skull-and-crossbones over a black heart. He did not believe in the efficacy of the French roundel after being attacked by a British Camel, and so added a tricoleur 'V' to his upper wing.

On the day that he reported to the *Escadrille N.65* Nungesser first 'beat-up' Nancy in a most spectacular fashion,

---

*Although it is widely believed that the stork was adopted as the mascot of the *Cigognes Escadrille* because of their Hispano engines, in fact the reverse is true. The stork was the group mascot even when they were flying Nieuports with Le Rhone engines and was retained after the switch to Hispano-engined Spads. After the war, when Hispano-Suiza were marketing motor-cars, they adopted the stork as their trade mascot.

flying in and out of church steeples and tall buildings, looping over the *Place* and charging up and down the *Boulevard* at an altitude of thirty feet. By the time he landed at his aerodrome, an official complaint from the townsfolk had already been laid on the Commanding Officer's desk. The latter, somewhat acidly, told his newest recruit to confine his aerobatics to enemy territory. Nothing daunted, Nungesser had his aircraft refuelled and forced several of his colleagues to accompany him to the nearest German airfield where, covered by his comrades, he repeated his performance.

In January of 1916 Nungesser was the victim of a serious accident when testing a new aeroplane. The joystick went through his mouth, dislocated his jaw and perforated his palate; in addition both his legs were broken. Yet within two months he was flying again, although he could move to and from his Nieuport only on crutches. Throughout April, Nungesser had to return to hospital for periodic treatment of his injuries. But while he was flying fresh wounds accumulated. His lip was slashed by an explosive bullet; his jaw was again broken when he inverted a damaged aircraft making a forced landing; and in another crash in No-man's Land, he dislocated his knee. In December he had to return to hospital to have all his fractures broken and reset, and was forced into a two month rest. But in May 1917 – the peak period of Albatros domination – Nungesser returned again to the fray in his personal Nieuport, now fitted with a Clerget engine of greater power.

Nungesser's return, in a period when Allied opposition was frail, and sometimes timid, was immediately noticed by the Germans. On 12 May a lone Albatros dropped a message challenging Nungesser to single combat that afternoon over Douai. Yet when he arrived at the appointed rendezvous, Nungesser found not one, but six of the enemy were waiting for him. But still he could not be killed; in the dogfight that followed this betrayal, Nungesser shot down two of his enemy (Paul Schweizer and Ernst Bittorf), and the rest scattered.

His health continued to deteriorate. Now two mechanics had to carry Nungesser into his cockpit for he could no longer manage even with his crutches. Throughout August he flew and fought, but his strength was *épuisé*. Unlike Guynemer who was also on the threshold of a nervous collapse, Nungesser allowed himself to be sent back to Paris on sick leave. On his flight home he was set on by a solitary Halberstadt. For over half an hour the two planes fought single-handed. Perhaps it was Nungesser's poor health, perhaps it was the exceptional skill of his opponent, but neither could gain the advantage. Finally, his fuel almost exhausted, Nungesser landed at Le

Touquet airfield and was surprised to see his unknown adversary land also and taxi towards him. When the two were side by side, the German waved gleefully, then opened his throttle and took off again. Curiously, this sporting gesture, so typical of the earlier days of aerial combat, was seen by Nungesser as a terrible humiliation and he was to spend hundreds of hours of his future flying life (for by now Nungesser had a roving commission and his attachment to N.65 was no more than nominal) searching for that same Halberstadt so that he could retrieve his honour.

That winter Nungesser skidded his Mors touring car on the icy road while driving back from Paris in the middle of the night. The car overturned and Nungesser was thrown out, once again breaking his jaw as well as suffering other injuries. But his faithful mechanic, Soldat Pochon, who was responsible for the maintenance of all Nungesser's planes, was trapped in the car and killed. Nungesser went back to hospital and for the remainder of the war his flying periods were punctuated by long spells in the care of doctors. While he was flying he struggled desperately to raise his score above that of his great rival, René Fonck, but in fact the highest that he could manage by Armistice was forty-five compared with Fonck's seventy-five (which made Fonck the Allied ace of aces), and the fifty-four which Guynemer had managed before his own death.

Although he survived, Nungesser, like so many of the aces, was diminished by his experiences and could not live in

Opposite Charles Nungesser standing beside his Nieuport. He was called 'the Indestructible' because he survived so many crashes, but after the war he was unable to adjust to peace-time conditions. In 1927 he disappeared during a flight across the Atlantic and no trace of him was found.

Below Nungesser in his Rolls-Royce. One of the accidents which most affected him occurred when he was returning by car to Paris with his faithful mechanic Pochon: Pochon was killed and Nungesser broke his jaw.

contentment without the stimulation of mortal danger. In search of his early inspiration he had built for himself, by Levasseur, a seaplane with which he intended – or so he claimed – to fly the Atlantic. Known as the *Oiseau Blanc* it was painted white overall but carried Nungesser's war-time insignia. The *Oiseau* was filled with enough fuel for the 4,000 mile flight and on a May morning, the anniversary of his greatest achievement, the single-handed defeat of the German ambush over Douai, Nungesser took off and pointed the *Oiseau* into the Atlantic haze. The seaplane flew due west until its engines could be heard no more. Like Guynemer, Nungesser disappeared without a trace.

René Fonck, who surpassed both Nungesser and Guynemer, was a man of very different mettle. He served in *SPA. 103*, an otherwise relatively undistinguished member of the *Cigognes* group, and was credited with three-quarters of the *Escadrille*'s kills. The secret of Fonck's success was different from those of his two nearest French rivals, and the reason is plain to see after an analysis of each man's temperament. Nungesser and Guynemer were highly-strung, emotional and impulsive, and

René Fonck, the Allied as well as the French ace of aces. Although he scored seventy-five victories, he was a cautious and conceited man who had none of Guynemer's charisma.

their victories were achieved in tempestuous flights, with the result often being very much in the balance. Fonck's victories were achieved in an altogether different way. He was a conceited, arrogant but thorough and painstaking pilot, and a superlative shot. Most of Fonck's later victims succumbed after Fonck had fired an absolute minimum number of rounds. This was made possible by Fonck's constant practice with machine-guns and carbines, and a careful analysis of German tactics and machines and how best to beat them both. By these means Fonck achieved the highest Allied score of the war, at minimum risk to himself, and also pulled off a unique feat: twice he shot down six German machines in a day, on 9 May and 26 September 1918. And on the second of these occasions, but for a jam in his machine-guns, he might well have despatched eight German machines. But despite his enormous success, Fonck never gained the emotional popularity Guynemer enjoyed.

Part Four

The End
of the Battles

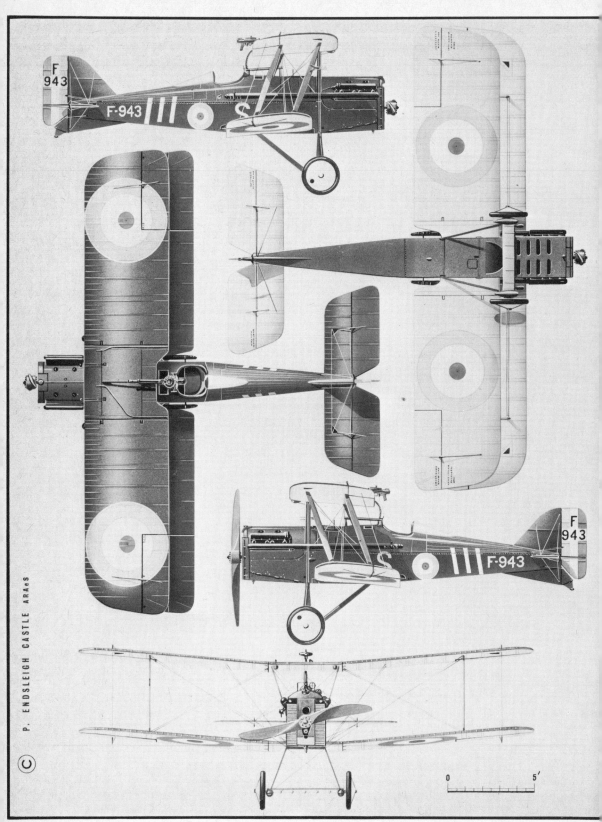

F
943

F-943

F
943

F-943

P. ENDSLEIGH CASTLE ARAeS

0   5'

SE 5A

Background 1918

The year 1918 opened with a clear Allied superiority in the air; the British SE 5As and Sopwith Camels and the French Spads had done their work well, and over the whole Western Front the Allied Air Forces maintained their tactical air offensive, overwhelming the German machines on their own side of the lines and allowing their own reconnaissance and observation machines to go about relatively unhindered. The one bright spot for Germany was the fact that she could wrest air superiority from the Allies locally by moving in a 'Circus', but this was costly in machines and trained personnel as the German fighters were still outclassed at this time. Although the French held the greater length of line on the ground, in the air it was the British that were the Germans' main opponents, as an examination of the forces arrayed against the British and French sectors clearly shows. At the end of March 1,680 German aircraft were operating in the British sector, and only 367 against the French. This was partly a result of large portions of the French front being 'quiet areas', partly the more aggressive ground policy displayed by the British, but partly also, the failing of the French tactical doctrine. Like the Germans the French had grouped together their best pilots in élite fighter units, leaving other fighter squadrons and all reconnaissance and observation units bereft of good pilots, and all the experience and morale they could have provided. This left these other squadrons so unaggressive and ineffectual that a few good German units sufficed to keep them in check, allowing most of the strength to be deployed against the British in the north.

More important, however, was the development of German offensive tactics in the field of army co-operation. We have already mentioned the growth of Schutzstaffeln (Protection flights) and Fliegerabteilungen-Infanterie (Infantry contact patrol), equipped at first with modified C types, pending the arrival of the J class machines. In the autumn of 1917, the Air Force authorities had foreseen the need for a lighter version of the J class, in fact something between the C and J classes, and ordered the CL class, which was to be able to act as escort for C class machines on reconnaissance flights, but also to fly ground attack missions. With the growing need for ground attack formations, a special title was introduced for the new units – Schlachtstaffeln

(Battle flights) and later, when such units had grown in size and importance, Schlachtgeschwadern *(Battle wings). The first major victory of the* Schlastas *(as they were abbreviated) was during the second half of the Battle of Cambrai in 1917, the world's first large scale tank offensive, when the German ground forces had been taken entirely by surprise and pushed back several miles, but had later been able to regain much of the lost ground with the help of the* Schlastas.

Throughout the winter and spring after the Battle of Cambrai, the Schlastas *were developed, strengthened, trained and brought as near as possible up to full complement with the latest equipment, the Halberstadt CL II and the Hannover CL II and III series. Just as the German Air Force had laid contingency plans against the arrival of huge American forces in France, so had the German army. Five large offensives for the spring and early summer of 1918 had been planned, to drive the Allies out of the war before America could make her weight felt. The* Schlastas *were to play a very important role in these offensives, the first of which, on the Somme, started on 20 March. The German tactics had been carefully worked out. It had been realized that the old style of offensive, preceded by a massive artillery bombardment, which threw away any chance of obtaining surprise, and carried out by slow-moving infantry, was useless. The new style was to have some of the elements of* Blitzkrieg *in it : the artillery bombardment was to be short and sharp, just to throw the enemy off its balance ; at H-hour, this was to become a creeping barrage, with swiftly-moving 'stormtroopers' moving in its wake, pressing on as fast as possible, ignoring strongpoints which could not be taken immediately, to take the enemy's artillery and to keep him off balance ; behind the stormtroopers were to come the ordinary infantry, to mop up and consolidate. Over the whole would operate the* Schlastas, *harrying the enemy with machine-gun fire and light bombs, and keeping the High Command informed of the progress of the ground troops, so that the barrage could be speeded up if necessary in the event of the stormtroopers' advance being faster than anticipated. It was essential that aircraft of the* Schlastas *operate in groups of about four to six aircraft, so that any commander could control his unit personally but still have a powerful offensive force, and that each section of the front be patrolled by a group, with a constant stream of replacements moving up to relieve those that had exhausted their ammunition or fuel. The* Schlastas, *therefore, fulfilled the roles of airborne light artillery in direct support of the ground troops, and as aerial liaison officers for the High Command.*

The plan worked brilliantly in the first offensive, though the British were finally able to halt the advance after it had outrun its services. But the four subsequent offensives were less successful

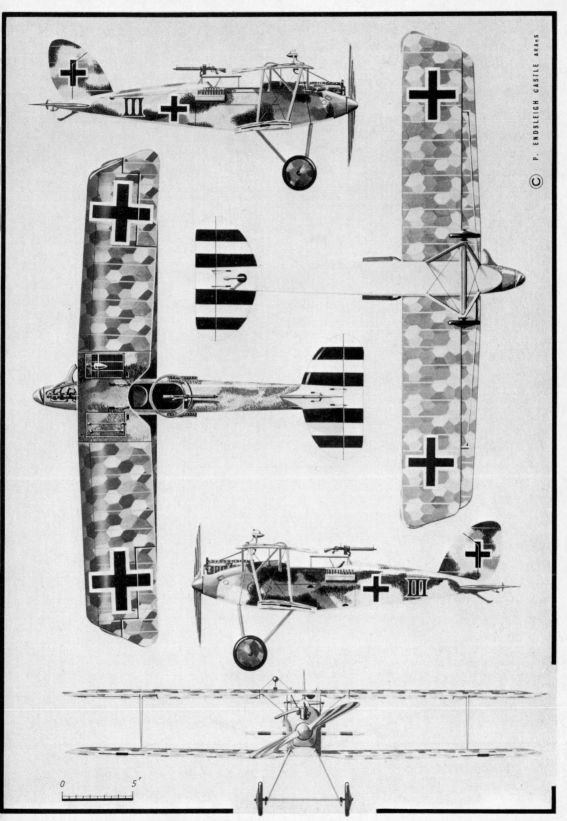

© P. ENDSLEIGH CASTLE ARAeS

Halberstadt CL II

as the Allies worked out plans of their own to halt both ground and air offensives. On the ground, defences were prepared in greater depth and with greater elasticity, while offensives were spotted before they started now that it was known what to look for. In the air, the Allies were forced to keep their fighters aloft even under the most hazardous conditions to check the Germans by shooting down their aircraft and harrying their ground troops, learning in combat the lessons which the Germans themselves had been able to prepare with greater time and thought. But finally the offensives were halted, the Germans were exhausted, and it was time for the Allies themselves, now with American aid, to go over on to the offensive.

This year, too, saw the impact of America on the air war. At the outbreak of the First World War in Europe in 1914, only sixty-five citizens of the United States held pilot's licences, and only thirty-five of these were in the Army. There was no air force worthy of the name, no machines, no operational theory, no command structure, no industrial specialization. Even more surprising, the tremendous enthusiasm which had kept aviation in a state of constant ferment in Europe was completely absent in the country of its origin.

The military value of aeroplanes had been totally discounted – it seemed – as a result of their performance in the Mexican War of 1913. The ten frail and unreliable Curtis biplanes that had accompanied the soldiers on that occasion had proved more of a liability than a help, breaking down, having forced landings and diverting soldiers and cavalry on the ground from their traditional tasks to aid the stranded pilots. This episode effectively closed the minds of the military who were naturally delighted to have their preconceived theories confirmed. As a result there had been absolutely no forward planning of aircraft design and development. Aeroplanes might fly the Channel (in one direction) but they were never going to fly the Atlantic. They could be ignored.

In July of 1914 an Act was passed by Congress which created the Aviation Section of the Signal Corps and authorized a strength of sixty officers and two hundred and sixty enlisted men. This was little more than formal recognition that the aeroplane existed and might possibly have a military use. But its status, as an ancillary of a subordinate branch, was emphasized by the tiny grant and the fact that only two commissioned ranks were envisaged in the pay scale. The previous year flying training had taken place at the airfield at College Park in Maryland – styled the Signal Corps Aviation School. But of the twenty-eight aircraft attached to the school, nine became total losses and over a quarter of the forty men who had received flying instruction lost their lives in accidents. By the time war broke out in Europe the eleven remaining Curtis-Wright 'pusher' aircraft at the school had been condemned on safety grounds and the Army had only five aeroplanes left, all in highly suspect condition. Flying training was discontinued and recruitment discouraged.

Fortunately for the United States, Glen Curtis continued to operate his private school at San Diego, California, using the 'J' or 'Jenny' – which was to be standardized as the Army's basic trainer in years to come.

In 1915 the Chief of the Signals section, General Scriven, recommended a force of eighteen squadrons (each of twelve planes). But no action was taken and even two years later when the United States actually entered the war, the Aviation Section had only 131 officers and 1,000 enlisted men. In its total of 250 aircraft there were none that could be rated as proper combat types in the sense that these had evolved by the standards of European fighting. There were only two air officers on the General Staff in Washington.

Within a few weeks of entering the war the American attitude to the Air Arm had changed completely, and the first steps were taken that were to secure for the United States a pre-eminence in the aero-industrial field that they have held until today. A programme was drafted calling for the production of 22,625 aeroplanes and 44,000 engines backed by an eighty per cent spares inventory. On 24 July Congress voted 640 million dollars for military aeronautics, the largest sum ever appropriated for a single purpose up to that time. The humble Aviation Section was scheduled for expansion to 345 combat squadrons with supporting formations. The American aircraft industry barely existed at this time. Its total production for the past ten years had been less than 800 aeroplanes. But its response was characteristic. The standard aero-engine, the Liberty, was designed by Jesse Vincent and J.G.Hall in five days. The prototype engine was complete with all accessories for testing in twenty-eight days. By the end of the war this engine was coming off the production line at 4,200 a week. The performance of Vincent and Hall, and of Douglas who adapted the DH 4 to take the Liberty engine in a single weekend, makes one regret that the United States had not the experience in designing aircraft that they had in designing machinery. Unfortunately, production plans were, as ever, over-optimistic, and very little of American manufacture saw combat in Europe. Even the DH 4, already mentioned, proved to have many shortcomings when tested in Europe, and was further delayed from its combat début while modifications were carried out. Even then it acquired an unenviable reputation as the 'flaming coffin'.

The United States' industrial capacity was more easily capable of tackling its enormous programme than was the Air Service in training the necessary crew. Predictably there was a flood of recruits, but ground schools, airfields, instructors and

training aircraft were woefully short. The authorities' require-
ments for a pilot would certainly have excluded many of the
European aces:

The candidate should be naturally athletic and have a reputation for
reliability, punctuality and honesty. He should have a cool head in
emergencies, good eye for distance, keen ear for familiar sounds,
steady hand and sound body with plenty of reserve; he should be quick-
witted, highly intelligent and tractable. Immature, high-strung, over-
confident, impatient candidates are not desired.

A further twenty-seven flying fields were constructed in the
United States to handle the training programme (only three had
existed at the outbreak of the war) but for advanced training
aircrew had to go to Europe where, in France, the United States
set up its own airfields and Aviation Instruction Centers.

It was not until the spring of 1918 that the American single-
seater ('Pursuit') squadrons were operational, although the 1st
Aero-Squadron had been in France since 1917 and, equipped with
Breguets, had been flying reconnaissance missions since the early
spring of 1918. The French and British commanders had hoped
to integrate the American squadrons piecemeal, as they were
formed, into existing allied units.

The American commanders on the other hand, wished to
preserve their independence and looked forward to the day when
their Air Force and Army could operate together as a whole.
With this in mind the first arrivals were kept in the Toul sector,
in the Vosges – a region that had seen no serious fighting at any
time since spring 1915. The pilots of these first two squadrons
(the 94th and 95th) had been subjected to a variety of delays and
obstructions by the authorities. The French had put them through
a whole sequence of advanced flying, gunnery and combat schools
and when they were finally issued with their new Spad single-
seaters they found that these had been sent down without guns.
Undaunted, the reckless Americans began to fly their patrols
unarmed – a practice which would have led to disaster in any other
sector of the front.

By the middle of June the American strength had risen to a
level where it was possible to constitute both an observation group
and a pursuit group and these, together with some French units,
moved north to the Château-Thierry sector. For a number of
historic reasons – notably the connection via the Lafayette
Escadrille *and the Americans already serving in French units*
who had been re-posted to all-American squadrons, and also the
influence of the French purchasing commissions – the United
States Air Force was chiefly influenced by the French and largely
ignored the British. This was regrettable as at this stage the
French Air Service was suffering a decline in morale. Now with

their move to Château-Thierry, the Americans found themselves flying against hardened professionals who enjoyed the advantages of experience and superior aircraft.

Just as the Lafayette squadron had first enjoyed a period of 'phoney war' so had the regular American units made the most of the Crillon Bar, the Château landings and the showy traditions of dress and behaviour that the flying community had established. But there were harsher lessons that could only be learned in combat; recognizing decoys, allowing for wind drift, vigilance against surprise, the proneness of guns to jam and controls to bind at freezing altitudes – these things took their toll of the Americans as they had of others before them. The 'Scarlet Scouts' and the 'Checkers' with their 'solid crimson leader' (presumably Jastas 11 and 34) soon burned their reputation across the American squadrons and losses mounted alarmingly.

But the Jastas moved up and down the front. Sometimes they would be absent for up to ten days at a time, and throughout the summer of 1918 the American strength mounted. By the time of the Saint Mihiel offensive in August, General William Mitchell, the American commander, had over 1,500 aeroplanes under his control. (Not all of these were exclusively United States formations and they included nine bomber squadrons from the RAF.) In the closing weeks of the war the American scores increased dramatically and when the Armistice was signed there were over forty-five American combat squadrons at the front with a strength of 740 aircraft. Against losses of 289 they claimed to have destroyed 781 Germans, a kill ratio of almost 3 : 1. The total strength of the American Air Force had already risen to over 14,000 aeroplanes and there is little doubt that it would have matched that of the Royal Air Force in 1919 and carried the major burden of air fighting from that time onward.

The American Air Force achievement is comparable only to the scale of their Space Programme in the 'sixties. Starting from nothing – or indeed a minus factor – in comparison with their competitors, they developed production, personnel, command and design structures on a scale and with a rapidity that towered over all others. Their contribution in the closing months of the war was significant not only in terms of morale, but in the way in which the hard-pressed Jastas were taxed beyond their strength by these brave new arrivals, and German air cover at critical points of the front became increasingly imperfect and unpredictable.

German strength in March 1918 had been 4,050 aircraft of all types, but wastage had been severe during the five German offensives. For example, they had lost 659 machines (including 182 single-seaters) between 20 March, the beginning of the Second Battle of the Somme, and 29 April, the date of the end of their second offensive, the Battle of the Lys. More important,

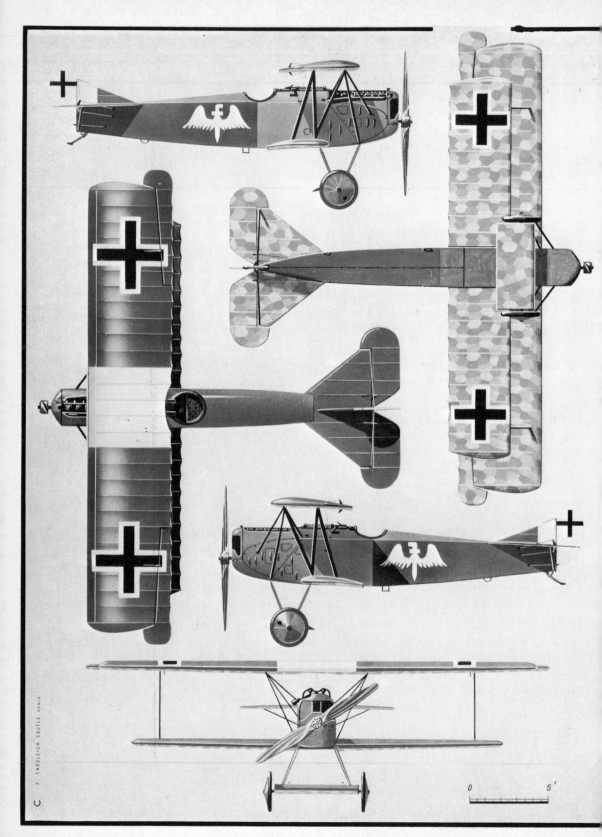

Fokker D VII

however, was the wastage in personnel, especially as many of those lost were irreplaceable men such as Manfred von Richthofen and the leaders and developers of the Schlastas. *Even if the German flying schools had been able to turn out the numbers needed as replacements, they could not provide the skills that years of active service had produced. On 8 June 1918 the German Air Force had only 2,551 pilots on its rolls.*

Two months later, when the final Allied offensives of the war started with the Battle of Amiens on 8 August (which Erich von Ludendorff, the German army's Chief-of-Staff, called 'the Black Day of the German army') the RAF had 1,782 aircraft (this figure rose to 1,799, including 747 fighters, by the time of the Armistice), the Americans 740 and the French over 3,000 of all types. From 8 August to the date of the Armistice, 11 November, the Allied armies rolled forward, covered in the air by forces modelled on the Schlastas *of the spring. There was nothing the Germans could do. Not only were the Germans outnumbered, they were also desperately short of fuel and lubricants, good quality linen to cover their machines, dope to tauten and air-proof them and skilled aircrew to make the best use of what they had. For all except the last the Germans had the unrelenting Allied blockade to thank, and for the last the offensive tactics pursued by Trenchard and other Allied Air Force leaders. It is ironic that it was during this period of defeat that Germany's best fighter of the war, the Fokker D VII, was available in its greatest numbers. But not even this magnificent fighter's performance could cope with the ever increasing and improving swarms of Allied aircraft, both fighters and two-seaters, crossing the retreating German lines.*

The war did not end with a climactic final battle in which the German Air Force was wiped out, but in its gradual decline and death from fuel starvation and inferiority of numbers. After years of struggle, at times against a foe superior in numbers and equipment, the Allied forces could rove with relative impunity over the collapsing German armies. The German Air Force had lost 5,853 men killed, 7,302 wounded and 2,751 missing and prisoner, together with 3,128 aeroplanes, 546 balloons and 26 airships. The Royal Flying Corps, Royal Naval Air Service and Royal Air Force had lost 6,166 men killed, 7,245 wounded and 3,212 missing and prisoner.

CHAPTER TEN

Vapour Trails

And two things have altered not
  Since first the world began –
The beauty of the wild green earth
  And the bravery of man.

Cameron Wilson (killed in action 1918)

With the shortening of the days in the late autumn of 1917, the hectic pace of aerial activity slackened and the Germans took stock of their position. Twice in the war a technical innovation, an aircraft far ahead of its adversaries, had given them the means to achieve a total superiority. Yet, from a combination of secondary factors this had each time eluded them. And just as the reign of the Fokker Eindekker with its synchronized Parabellum had been cut short by the arrival in the nick of time of the 'Fees' and the Nieuports, so the domination of the Albatros had been first shaken and then eclipsed by increasing numbers of SE 5As, Camels and Spads.

Although there were brilliant individual exceptions on the Allied side, it is probably true to say that the general level of tactical skill and flying expertise was higher in the closed fraternal societies of the *Jagdstaffeln*. Here the pilots were true specialists, their task was to seek out and destroy enemy planes free from the encumbrance of escort or ground-support roles; the manner in which they were rotated over different sectors of the front widened their experience; the way in which they were concentrated often gave them a local superiority of numbers in battle which did not reflect the overall strengths of the two sides; off-duty discussion of techniques and innovations was encouraged and there was a free and ready traffic of ideas between design staffs and the pilots in the field.

But it was now becoming apparent that their squadron equipment was a handicap and leading to an unnecessary wastage of good pilots. Neither the Albatros D V, which entered service in mid-1917, nor the Pfalz D III of autumn 1917 could match the developing SE 5A with a good pilot (in this case, Britain's top ace, with seventy-three victories, 'Mick' Mannock):

Bristol 7 2Bs setting off on a flight over the German lines in June 1918.

Above Members and
SE 5A's of No. 1
Squadron RAF at
Clairmarais
Aerodrome near
Ypres in July 1918.

Opposite German
airmen in Berlin
during the military
aircraft trials of
January 1918 when
the Fokker D VII was
displayed. From left
to right: Herr Seckatz
of the Fokker works,
Hermann Goering,
Lothar von
Richthofen, Hans
Kirschstein, Leutnant
Krefft, Friedrich
Mallinckrodt,
Leutnant Schubert.

. . . he had a fine set-to, while his patrol watched the master at work.
It was a wonderful sight. First they waltzed around one another
like a couple of turkey-cocks, Mick being tight on his adversary's
tail. Then the Pfalz [piloted by Leutnant Van Ira] half-rolled and
fell a few hundred feet beneath him. Mick followed, firing as soon
as he got into position. The Hun then looped – Mick looped too,
coming out behind and above his opponent. The Pfalz then spun –
Mick spun also, firing as he spun. This shooting appeared to me a
waste of ammunition. The Hun eventually pulled out; Mick was
fast on his tail – they were now down to 4,000 feet. The Pfalz now
started twisting and turning which was a sure sign of 'wind-up'.
After a sharp burst close up, Mick administered the *coup de grace*,
and the poor fellow went down headlong and crashed.

This was a remarkable exhibition, a marvellous show. I felt sorry
for the poor Pfalz pilot, for he put up a wonderful show of defensive
fighting. Had he only kept spinning right down to the ground, I
think he would have got away with it.

The *Jastas* needed a new single-seater and they needed it
urgently. As with the birth of the SE 5A, the key element in the
equation was the engine. The Mercedes 160 h.p. with honey-

comb radiator (which allowed a narrower frontal area and reduced drag) would, it was confidently expected, give this third generation of fighter planes climbing and fighting powers at high altitude significantly better than Allied equipment. Accordingly, in October of 1917, draft specifications were sent to the rival airframe manufacturers with instructions to tender for a new design to be built round the Mercedes 160 h.p. There was little time for the designers to develop their ideas. The *Flugzeug Wettewerg* (Evaluation Trials) had been fixed for the last ten days of January 1918 and the competing aircraft were to present themselves at the Adlershof airfield at Berlin where they were to be tried for 'general flying qualities, manœuvrability, diving ability, pilot's view, combat qualities' and other factors. A number of the leading aces were withdrawn from the *Jagdstaffeln* to take part in mock combats between the rival products. The autocratic Manfred von Richthofen would preside.

In spite of the biting winds and sub-zero temperatures, there was a considerable aura of chic about the affair. Fashionable ladies stood about dutifully on the tarmac, hands deep in their fur muffs, or held court on the back seats of their Mercedes Landaulettes, while directors and executives of the various business houses whose interests were at stake, busily ingratiated themselves with all those, notably the pilots, whose influence was critical. Exquisite food sent by Anthony Fokker in a special train from Holland (the blockade was

Fokker with Goering and Bruno Loerzer (left).

biting deeply in Germany at this time and basic foods were strictly rationed), quantities of champagne looted from Rheims and, of course, the company of all those ladies from the Opera House, were pressed on the pilots. But while they may have enjoyed these things, their decision seems to have been reached on strictly realistic grounds.

Of course we took favours from them all. It was no more than our due; what we had to give in return we had already paid and would pay again. All this luxury and softness reminded us that soon we would return to the bitter reality of blood and iron where so many of our comrades had already paid the price in full. What we had to decide was a matter of life and death – our own and those of our brothers who had remained behind fighting.

Designs had been submitted by AEG, Albatros, Aviatik, Fokker, Konder, Pfalz, Roland, Rumpler, Schütle-Lanz and Siemens Schuckert, but the aeroplane which stood out from all others was the new Fokker design, the D VII. A handsome single-seater with a lean flanked, 'razor-edge' fuselage, square wings and a very clean, although somewhat sinister silhouette, emphasized by its slender bracing which was almost invisible from some angles against the light. Maximum speed was 118 m.p.h.; climb to 10,000 feet was $9\frac{1}{2}$ minutes compared with the SE 5A's 10 minutes 20 seconds and the Camel's 8 minutes 10 seconds. The D VII's most vital asset, however, was its ability to hang on its propeller at altitude, where the Allied machines would have stalled or have had to lose height.

Production orders followed at once with only minor modifications to fuselage lengths and fin. Nine weeks later the

first allocations were made to *Jagdgeschwader 1*, and word began to spread of the new Fokker's outstanding qualities.

Rudolph Stark of *Jasta 35* told how:

Six Fokkers . . . great rejoicing throughout the *Staffel*. An Albatros, two Pfalz and three Rolands are wheeled out for exchange. Now comes the burning question, who is to fly the new machines – I decide the last to join the Staffel must be the ones to wait. I report to the Technical Officer who presents the necessary documents to make us the happy owners of six Fokkers which are waiting in the hangar. I climb into the cockpit which wears an unfamiliar aspect; the engine roars; the ground rushes away from under me. Swiftly we rise. The machines climb wonderfully and answer to the slightest movement of the controls. We land and put our treasures safely away in the hangars. The painter marks them with the *Staffel* badge, the arrowhead on the wings, then paints the fuselages with the coloured bands that identify the individual pilots. He takes particular care with my machine embellishing my lilac stripe with narrow black edges. Only then do the machines really belong to us.

It was not long before that stark, square-rigged outline became an object of foreboding to the RFC. Cases of turning away and avoiding combat, of 'suspected engine failure' or 'guns jamming' came to be recorded with increased frequency as they had in the first days of the Albatros.

We got into a dogfight this morning with the new brand of Fokkers and they certainly were good. They had big red stripes on the fuselage diagonally so they must have been von Richthofen's old Circus. There were five of us and we ran into five Fokkers at 15,000 feet. We both started climbing of course – and they out-climbed us. We climbed up to 20,500 feet and couldn't get any

The Fokker D VII. In the autumn of 1917 the German authorities invited manufacturers to submit single-seater fighter prototypes in the hope of finding an aircraft that could regain ascendancy over the Allied fighters on the Western Front. In the trials the following January the Fokker D VII was unanimously acclaimed the best plane and was put into mass production.

higher. We were practically stalled and these Fokkers went right over our heads and got between us and the lines. They didn't want to dogfight, but tried to pick off our rear men. Inglis and Cal were getting a pretty good thrill when we turned back and caught one Hun napping. He half rolled slowly and we got on his tail. Gosh, its unpleasant fighting at that altitude. The slightest movement exhausts you.

Your engine has no pep and splutters; it's hard to keep a decent formation, and you lose 500 feet on a turn. The Huns came in from above and it didn't take us long to fight down to 12,000 feet. We put up the best fight of our lives, but these Huns were just too good for us. Cal got a shot in his radiator and went down and Webster had his tailplane shot to bits and his elevator control shot away. He managed to land with his stabiliser wheel, but cracked up. I don't know what would have happened if some Dolphins from 84 hadn't come up and the Huns beat it. I think we got one that went down in a spin while Cal was shooting at it, but we couldn't see it crash. I got to circling with one Hun, just he and I, and it didn't take me long to find out that I wasn't going to climb above this one. He began to gain on me and then did something I've never heard of before. He'd been circling with me and he'd pull around and point his nose at me and open fire and just hang there on his prop and follow me around with his tracer. All I could do was keep on turning the best I could. If I'd straightened out he'd have had me cold as he already had his sights on me. If I tried to hang on my prop that way, I'd have gone right into a spin. But this fellow just hung right there and sprayed me with lead like he had a hose. All I could do was to watch his tracer and kick my rudder from one side to the other to throw his aim off. This war isn't what it used to be. (Account by Lieutenant John M. Grider.)

But if their equipment had been up-graded, the human element in the *Jastas* was now in decline. Frankenberg, returning from his second convalescence after wounding, found '. . . deep changes in the Staffel, like an ancient tapestry which has been darned and patched until, though it hangs in the same pattern, few fragments of the original cloth can be recognized'.

Their bravery was unquestioned, but bitterness and cynicism multiplied as the fighting front contracted and the pressure of the Allies continued without cease. Richthofen had died on 21 April 1918, shot down by a Canadian, Captain A.R. Brown of 208 Squadron, flying a Sopwith Camel. The roll of those who succeeded him as Commander of the *Jagdgeschwader* rang with the names of aces - Wilhelm Reinhard, Erich Loewenhardt and Hermann Goering. Their life expectancy was measured in days. The Circuses still daubed their old warpaint (after Richthofen's death JG 2 switched from red to royal blue fuselages and these were boldly emblazoned – lightning for Graven, an arrow for Kurt Wolff, skull and crossbones for Georg von Hantelmann, a branding iron for Oliver, Frieherr von Beaulieu–Marconnay). But used again and again, driven to the point of exhaustion, the Circuses now fought without either mercy or hope.

It is fitting to close these accounts with the epic story of the last flight of Major William Barker who had survived in the Royal Flying Corps since 1915, when he had transferred from the machine-gun section of the Canadian Mounted Rifles. Barker had served on the ground in the Battle of Ypres when the Germans had used poison gas for the first time on the Western Front and the Canadian soldiers held the breach when the French ran away, by standing on the parapet of their trench line (where the gas was thinnest) with no more protection over their mouths than handkerchiefs dipped in a solution of chlorate and water. Barker's first post was as observer in a BE 2C, and here his skill and accuracy with a machine-gun quickly proved their worth and he shot down an Albatros on his fourth flight. He was then sent for training as a pilot and again showed exceptional aptitude, soloing after only fifty-five minutes of dual instruction.

Barker's first charge was the dangerous and unwieldy RE 8 and he was nearly killed standing one on its nose after making a damaged landing. Transferred to Camels he brought his score up to nine aircraft before being posted back to England as an instructor, but with the collapse of the Italian front at Caporetto there was an urgent need for British reinforcements and the flying schools were gleaned for volunteers to accompany the expeditionary army. Barker stayed in Italy until the end of the summer, by which time the war in that theatre had effectively ended, and then returned to the Flying Combat School at Hounslow, to which he had been appointed Commander.

But although the war in Italy was over and the Western Front now saw the German army in decline, the enemy air force remained extremely formidable. In all-round terms the new Fokker D VII was the best fighter in the sky. The German Air Force though smaller in terms of general quality was still superior to that of the Allies. It is probably also true that human material recruited into the RFC was below the standards of 1915 and 1916 just as was the case in the army itself, and the casualty figures remained disturbing. Using this excuse, but doubtless from a private nostalgia for the thrills of combat, Barker arranged to become temporarily attached to 201 Squadron. Although 201 was equipped with Camels, Barker himself brought out the latest fighter, the Sopwith

Sincerely yours
W. A. Bishop—

Snipe, which was intended to out-perform the Fokker D VII.

For the first three weeks of October, Barker served with 201 Squadron, sometimes sortie-ing in their company and sometimes flying as a lone wolf, and in this period he brought his total score up to forty-six planes. But on 26 October he was ordered home, taking-off the following day with his tanks full for the flight to England.

After about twenty minutes' flying time, Barker noticed a Rumpler two-seater at 2,000 feet to his north-end and diverted from his homeward course to intercept it. He had been lured, as so many of the aces ultimately were, by the prospect of one more vulnerable two-seater to add to his score. And, just as in their cases, Barker allowed his concentration to be deflected for seconds too long. As he followed the shattered Rumpler down to its death, Barker suddenly felt himself under fire, and simultaneously an incendiary bullet practically severed his right thigh, smashing the bone. Giving full left rudder (excruciating pain prevented him using the right pedal, he was thus limited to turning to one side only) Barker banked round and found himself flying head-on into the full strength of *Jagdgeschwader 3* whose four *Jastas* (*Nos. 2, 26, 27,* and *36*) were in stepped-up formation from 8,000 feet – in all some sixty Fokkers, all D VIIs!

There could be no escape. For an instant Barker's audacity in flying straight through them seems to have surprised the Germans; he succeeded in shooting down the plane which had first attacked him, and latched on to the tail of another which exploded in flames after the second burst. But once the Germans had satisfied themselves that there were no other English aircraft in sight and that Barker was truly alone, they fell into an attack technique which could only have one end; they took it in turns to attack him from different sides in clusters of five with one above and one below so that each time the Snipe evaded, it would offer a target either in a loop or a dive. After a few minutes during which time his aircraft was hit by over three hundred bullets, Barker was wounded again, this time in the left leg, so that he was almost incapable of operating the rudder controls and had to manoeuvre the aircraft on the joystick and throttle alone. He had now lost so much blood from the original wound in his right thigh that he fainted and the Snipe went into a spin. However, the rush of air and unfamiliar gyrating motion must have revived Barker for after falling some 6,000 feet, he instinctively pulled the Snipe out of the spin, although there could be no escape from his pursuers who were following him down and whose numbers had indeed been increased by the lowest of the four *Jastas* (*No. 27*) which had been flying at 8,000 feet.

Opposite William Barker, a Canadian soldier who transferred to the RFC in 1915 and became an expert pilot. On 27 October 1918 he fought his epic single-handed battle against more than sixty enemy aircraft.

The Sopwith Snipe, which was hoped to be the answer to the Fokker D VII. It was slightly larger than the Camel which it was designed to replace and handled beautifully.

Barker had now given up any thought of coming out of the fight alive, and half delirious with pain and loss of blood would try and ram his enemies when they came close enough. The Snipe still had some ammunition in its guns and Barker managed to shoot down one more Fokker before his left elbow was shattered and he became unconscious for the second time. Again the crazy spin which followed made it difficult for the Fokkers both to follow him down and shoot straight. Miraculously, and almost at ground level, Barker managed to straighten out for the last time. He was now only intermittently conscious and without control through any limb except his right wrist. Still travelling at almost maximum speed Barker tried to put the Snipe down in a field behind the British trench line. It hit the turf at 90 m.p.h, tore off its undercarriage, slid and bounced, shedding fabric and spars for two hundred yards and then turned over. Providentially, it did not catch fire, and the Highland Light Infantry who pulled Barker from the wreckage were astonished to find that his heart was still beating although the cockpit was awash with blood and both legs were held on by sinew alone.

Ernest Udet, the
second highest
scoring German ace.
During the Second
World War he rose
to be chief of the
Technical Office of
the *Luftwaffe*.

Barker was unconscious for ten days but ultimately recovered the full use of his limbs in time to attend the parade at which he was awarded the Victoria Cross by the King. With the exception of Mannock's slaughter of the Aviatik Training flight in 1917, Barker's performance had produced the highest score (four aircraft) in the shortest time (forty minutes) of any contest in the First World War. It was an act of incredible heroism and a fitting finale to the war in the air which came to an end twelve days later.

With what were the flyers left? Memories and nostalgia of an extraordinary power, that could never be deleted; a special bond that united all, even friend and foe, who had flown without a parachute, with the dive-wind on their cheeks, to the harsh rattle of machine-gun fire.

Some of those who survived went on to achieve eminence in the Second World War. Arthur Gould Lee and Norman MacMillan, both of whose memoirs have been quoted in this book, held high positions; Ernst Udet became chief of the technical office of the *Luftwaffe* where he was responsible for

developing the dive-bomber and (ironically) retarding the jet fighter; Goering rose to be the second most powerful man in Germany under Hitler. The summer of 1918 took a grievous toll of the old aces. Wolff died in Richthofen's own plane. Mannock was lured to his death by an apparently defenceless two-seater. McCudden, whose elder brother had been killed in May 1915, and his younger brother in March 1918, was himself killed in a take-off crash a few weeks before the Armistice. Lothar von Richthofen survived the war but was killed in a civilian aircraft at Fuhlsbüttel in 1922. 'Moritz' had been bequeathed by Richthofen to Gestenberg, who looked after the dog, and after the war he survived in Holland to a ripe old age.

Opposite The grave of Albert Ball.

Civilian accidents claimed many among those adventurous spirits who could not settle down but followed their calling in worn-out and unserviceable aircraft, stunting and mail-flying in remote parts of the world. William Barker's ninth life came up, and was forfeit in a take-off accident at Ottawa in 1930, twelve years after his single-handed duel with the Circus. Jean Navarre, taken out of a mental home to participate in a French victory parade, killed himself practising for a display where he intended to fly through the Arc de Triomphe. Cecil Lewis went as far as China, but the charmed life which had protected him since 1915 continued to do so and he survived to ferry Spitfires in the Second World War, leaving us one sentence that epitomizes all those memories and evocations that conjure up the bitter romance of dog fighting:

The way the earth looked, falling; swallowing to stop deafness at altitude; the scream of wires; stars between wings; grass blown down when engines were run up; the smell – of dope, and castor oil, and varnish in new cockpits; moonlight shining on struts; the gasps before the dive; machine-guns.

Appendix I

Comparative weights and performance of leading combat aircraft of the First World War

	Engine	Weight (lbs) Empty	Loaded	Maximum Ground
Fokker Monoplane EI 1915–16	80 h.p. EI	787	1,239	81
Bristol Scout C and D 1915–16	80 h.p. Le Rhone	766	1,195	92.7
BE2, 2A and 2B 1914–16	70 h.p. Renault	1,050	1,650	73
Sopwith 1½ Strutter 1915–17	110 h.p. Clerget	1,308	2,223	91
Sopwith Triplane 1916–18	130 h.p. Clerget	1,101	1,541	114
Sopwith Pup 1916–17	80 h.p. Le Rhone	787	1,225	111.5
Spad XIII CI 1916–18	220 h.p. Hispano-Suiza	1,245	1,807	—
RE8 1916–18	140 h.p. RAF 4a	1,622	2,592	—
Bristol Fighter 1916–18	190 h.p. Falcon I	1,727	2,753	110
Albatros D V 1916–18	160 h.p. Mercedes	1,367	1,874	—
SE5A 1917–18	200 hp. Hispano-Suiza	1,400	1,953	131
Sopwith Camel 1917–18	130 h.p. Clerget	950	1,482	118
Fokker D VII 1917–18	160 h.p. Mercedes	1,474	2,112	124 130*
Pfalz D XII 1917–18	170 h.p. D IIIa	1,444	1,984	115

*Later marks

d (m.p.h.) at 10,000 ft	Time taken to climb to 10,000 ft	Service ceiling (feet)	Endurance (hours)	Number built
—	Over 40 minutes	—	$1\frac{1}{2}$	Approx 65
36.5	21 mins 20 secs	15,500	$2\frac{1}{2}$	374
—	—	10,000	3	Approx 180
87.5	29 mins 30 secs	16,000	3	Approx 5,990
07.5	11 mins 50 secs	22,000	$2\frac{1}{2}$	Approx 150
04.5	14 mins 25 secs	17,500	3	Approx 1,800
32	8 mins	24,000	2	8,472
93	22 mins	13,500	$4\frac{1}{4}$	Approx 4,300
01	14 mins 30 secs	16,000	$3\frac{1}{4}$	Approx 3,528
03 08*	14 mins 8 secs 12 mins 30 secs*	20,000 22,500*	$3\frac{1}{2}$	Approx 526 Approx 1,200*
26	10 mins 20 secs	22,000	3	Approx 5,000
12.5	10 mins 35 secs	20,000	3	Approx 5,500
14 24*	14 mins 9 mins 20 secs*	— 23,000*	— $2\frac{1}{2}$*	Approx 400 Approx 950*
05	11 mins	20,000	2	Approx 850

Appendix 2

Comparative chart showing when leading combat aircraft were in operation during the First World War

	1914	1915
British ● Prototype **French** ■ Operational **German**	J F M A M J J A S O N D	J F M A M J J A S O N D
Fokker Monoplane	⊘⊘⊘⊘⊘⊘⊘⊘ /////////	//////////////////////
Bristol Scout	██████	██████████████████████
BE 2	███████	
De Havilland DH 2		●●●████
Sopwith 1½ Strutter (RNAS)		●
Nieuport 17		
Roland C11		⊙⊙⊙
Sopwith Triplane (RNAS)		
Albatros D1-111		
Sopwith Pup (RNAS)		
Spad XIII C1		
RE 8		
De Havilland DH 4		
Gotha G111		
Bristol Fighter		
SE 5		
De Havilland DH 5		
Albatros D v		
SE 5A		
Sopwith Camel		
Pfalz D 111		
Fokker Triplane		
Sopwith Dolphin		
Siemens Schuckert		
Fokker D VII		
Fokker D VIII		
Pfalz D XII		
Sopwith Snipe		

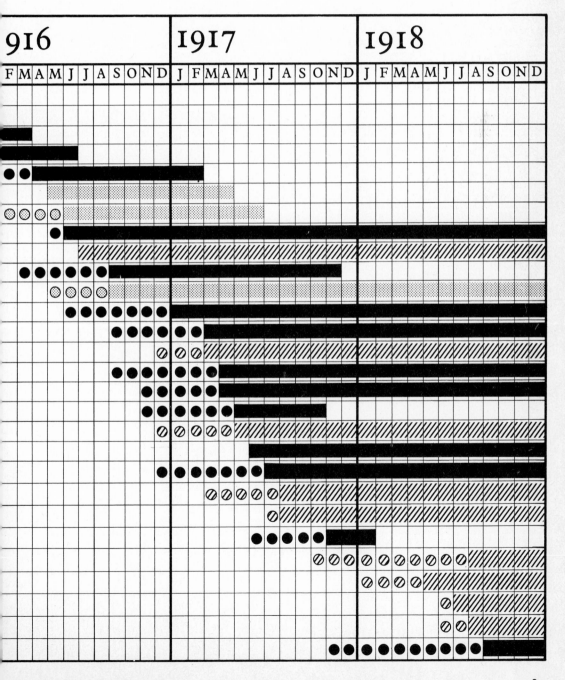

Index